POLAR SHIFT: THE ARCTIC SUSTAINED

POLAR SHIFT: THE ARCTIC SUSTAINED

JOSEPH F. C. DiMENTO

Anthem Press
An imprint of Wimbledon Publishing Company
www.anthempress.com

This edition first published in UK and USA 2023
by ANTHEM PRESS
75–76 Blackfriars Road, London SE1 8HA, UK
or PO Box 9779, London SW19 7ZG, UK
and
244 Madison Ave #116, New York, NY 10016, USA

First published in the UK and USA by Anthem Press in 2022

British Library Cataloguing-in-Publication Data
A catalogue record for this book is available from the British Library.

Library of Congress Cataloging-in-Publication Data
Names: DiMento, Joseph F., author.
Title: Polar shift : the Arctic sustained / by Joseph F.C. DiMento.
Description: London; New York, NY : Anthem Press, an imprint of Wimbledon Publishing Company, 2022. | Includes bibliographical references and index. |
Identifiers: LCCN 2022000095 | ISBN 9781839989223 (paperback) | ISBN 9781839983290 (pdf) | ISBN 9781839983306 (epub)
Subjects: LCSH: Environmental policy–Arctic regions–International cooperation. | Environmental protection–Arctic regions–International cooperation. | Sustainability–Arctic regions. | Arctic regions–Environmental conditions.
Classification: LCC GE190.A75 D56 2022 |
DDC 363.7/052509113–dc23/eng20220223
LC record available at https://lccn.loc.gov/2022000095

ISBN-13: 978-1-83998-922-3 (Pbk)
ISBN-10: 1-83998-922-X (Pbk)

Cover image: Jökulsárlón, Iceland-Photo by Roxanne Desgagnés

This title is also available as an e-book.

CONTENTS

NEWS FROM THE ARCTIC SEPTEMBER 2035

A daily report of news and events in the Arctic region compiled from international news sources.

The United Nations reported that financial contributions of countries to the Assisted Environmental Migration Fund had once again missed their commitment goals.

The high temperature yesterday in Deadhorse, Alaska, was 91.5°F (www.alaskaweather.com).

Iceberg of Reykjavik announced on Tuesday that there were no plans for glacier walks in Iceland again this year and that the company would be focusing on volcano watches and history tours.

Municipal authorities reported that the population of Nuuk, Greenland, surpassed that of Tromsø, Norway and Fairbanks, Alaska—reaching 75,000 in the latest census.

A High North webpage reported that a polar bear sighting in Lapland last December has been questioned.

After a lull of almost five years, two more Arctic cultural practices and expressions were inscribed on the UNESCO's List of Intangible Cultural Heritage (https://ich.unesco.org/en/lists).

The caribou population in the Arctic tundra has stabilized after decades of decline.

The price of Arctic crude oil hit a new low at 0.5 bitcoins per barrel.

Another Russian icebreaker, this one the *Arktika*, will be converted to a cruise line ship. Tour company experts question whether there will be sufficient interest in boarding a former nuclear-powered vessel for pleasure.

The beach shore off Kangertussuaq, Greenland, has receded several centimeters this year according to the federal webpage of Greenland.

The Arctic Council has completed its evaluation of programs to rid the region of plastic debris. Its conclusion was cautiously positive (www.arcticcouncil.com).

The population of another species of fish, the Bering Wolffish, has collapsed in the Central Arctic—this while record catches of salmon were recorded, the *Central Arctic Ocean Daily* reported.

The *Serenity Cruise Reunion* ship again broke the record for travel time though the Northwest Passage.

Greenland sand sales continued to boom related to new stability in the Middle East.

The number of indigenous peoples elected to legislative bodies in Arctic countries leveled off at the national level, but increased significantly at the state, provincial and other subnational levels.

ACKNOWLEDGMENTS

When I was a little boy, my older brother Lou and I would huddle late in the afternoon, the February sun having set, in an igloo we had built. Construction began with snowballs which we rolled and rolled until they were as big as refrigerators. We shaped them, hauled them one atop the other, carved a front door and then hollowed out the interior room. The temperature was perhaps 18°F/-8°C or—one time 22°F below 0/-30°C. Sometimes, not often, we saw the aurora borealis, the Northern Lights. It snowed a lot; some years, we received 125 inches (318 centimeters). One year it reached 192 inches (488 centimeters).

In winter, we also got out the rubber hose and made an ice rink in front of our house so we could play hockey with our little friends. We lived in Syracuse, New York, latitude 43.0481° N. This wonderful youth may explain why I love the Arctic. It seems, in many places, very familiar—even the hats and the gloves and the weird boots....

I thank our mother for letting us, no, encouraging us, to play outside. I thank Syracuse for giving us that outside. Many colleagues and friends helped me deepen my love and knowledge of the Arctic. They have, in so many ways, contributed to the rich, inspiring and informative trips I have taken. From my flying over the blue ice of Greenland, praying in wooden churches in Norway, tripping on the hard ice of astonishingly fast melting glaciers in Iceland to exploring museums of deep cultural and historic knowledge in Nuuk and Rovaniemi, seeing the city of Kiruna, where big parts of the urban place had to be moved because of a mine...to dining on reindeer and having a taste of whale, and char, to driving from where the dump was to where it will be in Iqaluit—an unattractive jaunt made lovely as we passed by the starkly beautiful and almost empty campgrounds of Nunavut. To heading North on carless dirt roads with a Chinese family to the Arctic Circle in Alaska. To gazing from 30,000 feet onto the glorious stark beauty of Canada. To learning, after a tour down in the permafrost, of the stubborn hopes of a return to Soviet era economic success in Siberia. To chatting with passionate Arctic advocates over expensive beer (everywhere in the Arctic)…

I deeply appreciate the wise advice and friendships of Arctic experts Oran Young, Timo Koivurova, Tullio Scovazzi, Tore Henriksen, Michael Byers, Brian Israel, Betsy Baker, Fran Ulmer, Craig Fleener, Jessica Shadian, Bob Lutz, Michael LeVine and Tom Leshine; Seth Davis provided important guidance on indigenous peoples' perspectives.

I would like to thank Fulbright Canada, especially Michael Hawes and Donoleen Hawes; the Canadian Consulate, Los Angeles, especially Sue Garbowitz; the Finnish Consulate, Los Angeles; and the Swedish Consulate, San Francisco, especially Barbro Osher, who provided important introductions and assistance with logistics.

Funding came from the School of Law, University of California Irvine (UCI), and its Center for Land Environment and Natural Resources (CLEANR) as well as from the Newkirk Center for Science and Society. CLEANR's Melissa Kelly and Elizabeth Taylor contributed to several of the background research materials for the book. They were assisted by UCI law students Tyler Shum, Kristen Kido and Kaitlin O'Donnell.

The Arctic University of Norway in Tromsø (UiT) and the Arctic Center of the University of Lapland at Roveniemi, Finland, generously provided office space and support when I visited the region. I thank the over 200 respondents to the UCI Arctic Survey on the future of the Arctic environment (described in Chapter 1) for their generous and often detailed thoughts and comments. Many respondents chose to remain anonymous, and there are too many to list all those who did not. Their opinions contribute to the understandings I have attempted to pass on in this book.

Similarly, I appreciate the time and insights supplied by the dozens of interviewees in federal, state, provincial, municipal and tribal offices throughout the Arctic, in Nuuk, Ottawa, Iqaluit, Tromsø, Rovaniemi, Yakutsk and Fairbanks, elected officials and agency staff. Interviews—many formal, some informal—were conducted with indigenous hosts and indigenous leaders, hunters and fishers, academics in almost all Arctic specializations, officials of the Arctic Council and other Arctic organization, staff members of consulates and an embassy as well as leaders of international NGOs. I also learned much from conversations with Arctic people during my innumerable daily interactions.

The UCI Center for Statistical Consulting Services helped make sense of the thousands of individual answers to the Arctic Survey.

It is perhaps surprising to people who see only the resulting book with an author's name to realize how important research teams are to a research and writing project. I have had the great fortune of being assisted by Christine Wendel, Margaret Woodruff, Kaitlin O'Donnell as well as by librarians Jessica Pierucci, Christina Tsou and Dianna Sahhar.

Julianne Ohlander and Naomi Aguilar provided outstanding support in the many activities that informed this book. John Whiteley, always supportive and generous and optimistic about my work, is an ongoing inspiration to act to promote sustainability of the planet. A number of anonymous reviewers of the manuscript helped clarify and tighten parts of the text, and I am deeply grateful to them.

1

INTRODUCTION: THE REGION OF THE CENTURY

When you hear "Arctic," what comes to mind? The North Pole, polar bears, reindeer, the midnight sun, the sunless day? Or the word may evoke permafrost, thunderous melting ice, native people, courageous explorers, oil exploiters, new luxury cruise ships, people seeking a more pristine home. If you live in the Arctic, the question may mean little, as for people who live elsewhere, when they hear North American or Mediterranean or African…what do you envision? But for those who do not live in the Arctic, trying to capture the full diversity and breath of this place is a mammoth task. Although it is difficult to appreciate the region with summary statements, to get some overall context a few facts are useful.

Only .051 percent of humanity calls the Arctic home. The Arctic Ocean around them covers 14 million square kilometers/almost 5.5 million square miles, the size of Antarctica. Superimposed on the United States, it would overlap it 1.5 times. Including land, it is 37 million square kilometers (over 14 million square miles). Four million people, including members of dozens of indigenous peoples' groups, live in the Arctic. Although the human population is very small, the number of distinct peoples in the Arctic is in the hundreds, including indigenous peoples who have called it home for centuries.[1] With them, walrus, seals, reindeer, caribou, seabirds and 150 species of fish live. In all, 21,000 known species of all kinds are found there, some new and invasive.

The Arctic includes tens of thousands of islands—some of which have zero population, some of which have seasonal populations and some of which have populations year-round. The Arctic encompasses all of the time zones. There are cities in the Arctic—some very industrial—of many thousands of people. North of the Arctic Circle there are 10 cities with 30,000 or more people, but many Arctic communities are very small. The most northern settlement in the world is there.

Permafrost, the once thought forever-frozen layer under the Earth's surface—soil, gravel and sand bound together by ice—covers large parts of the Arctic—in some places up to 1,000 meters, or more than six-tenths of a mile deep.[2] There are some wetlands, sparsely dotting the immense region; so too are boreal forests of coniferous trees.[3] And the Arctic is home to important minerals: gemstones, nickel, copper, platinum, apatite, tin, diamonds, gold, lead, zinc, copper and rare earth elements.[4] One-fifth of the world's oil and gas resources are in the Arctic. There is much sand and gravel.

Unlike Antarctica, which is land surround by water, the Arctic is more than a sea surrounded by land: it is a region. But there is no universally accepted definition of what the region includes. It may be demarcated by the tree line: the northernmost boundary where trees grow. It may be defined by temperatures: the southernmost location where the mean temperature of the warmest month of the year is below 10°C (50°F). The Arctic Circle currently begins at 66°33′43″ N (its precise coordinates depend on the tilt of the Earth's axis which changes with time). The North Pole is at 90° N, 0° E.[5] For certain purposes, the Arctic is defined by memberships in international or regional organizations.

To understand the environment of the sea and think about its future requires knowing about the land that touches that sea, that pours people and their vessels, effluents and waters as well as sediments into it. That land is, first, the territory of the Arctic Five—the countries that have Arctic coastline. These are the littoral states: Norway, Greenland through its relationship with Denmark of which it is for the time being a constituent county, the United States, Canada and Russia. The three other Arctic nations are Sweden, Iceland and Finland whose economies and cultures are heavily influenced by the Arctic, its weather, its climate, its indigenous and at least some nomadic peoples. These nations also have legal power over activities in the Arctic Sea under international law. The larger group is known as the Arctic Eight. At 62°00′ N, the Faroe Islands between Norway and Iceland, are about 4° S of the official boundary of the Arctic Circle. But its government has an Arctic policy, and the Faroe Islands is part of a delegation called Denmark/Greenland/Faroe Islands. New land areas, mainly islands, are regularly found in the Arctic. The Russian Navy in recent years has discovered over 30, along with bays, capes and straits, including new islands in the archipelagos of Novaya Zemlya and Franz Josef Land. One of these is 54,500 square meters or about 65,000 square yards.[6]

The Arctic coastline is about 45,000 kilometers or about 28,000 miles long. One starting point for thinking about the ocean element of the region is to realize that it is part of "one single interconnected ocean system: The Arctic, the Atlantic Ocean, the Indian Ocean and the Pacific Ocean."[7] The

Arctic itself is the world's smallest and most shallow: its average (mean) depth is 1,205 meters or just shy of 4,000 feet. The deepest point in the Arctic is the Molloy Deep at 5,607 meters or 18,400 feet. The ocean part of the Arctic is the waters semi-enclosed by the North American and Eurasian landmasses. The ocean includes many bodies of water known, depending on where one lives, by familiar names: however, which exactly are Arctic is not agreed upon by all experts. Generally, they are the Baffin Bay, the Barents Sea, the Beaufort Sea, the Chukchi Sea, the East Siberian Sea, the Greenland Sea, Hudson Bay, Hudson Strait, the Kara Sea, the Laptev Sea, the White Sea, the Northwest Passage and other tributary water bodies.

Looking at a detailed map is another way of getting a sense of how the Arctic is a place. The shortest distance between Russia's mainland and mainland Alaska is about 55 miles: the Bering Strait of the Pacific. But looking closely, in the Bering Strait are two small islands: Big Diomede and Little Diomede. Big Diomede is Russian; Little Diomede is part of the United States; 2.5 miles or about four kilometers separate these small places. A good snowmobiler could move from one nation to the other in a minute and a half.[8] Now look to Lapland, the region in the Arctic describing Norway, Sweden and Finland and parts of Russia. From Northern Finland to Sweden or Norway or Russia is no more than several miles. Twenty-five kilometers or about 16 miles separate Franklin Island in Greenland and Ellesmere Island in Canada.

But distances are also great in the Arctic. Shipping routes are the Northeast Passage, which goes along the coasts of Norway, Russia and Alaska including from west to east the Barents Sea, Kara Sea, Laptev Sea, East Siberian Sea and Chukchi Sea, and it includes the Northern Sea Route (NSR), the Russian section between the Atlantic and Pacific Ocean. Along the Russian coast, the route is immensely long, extending from Siberia and the Far East, from the Atlantic to the Pacific. Another is the Northwest Passage along the northern coast of North America which spans 900 miles.

The Arctic has been persistently cold, and its temperature has not ranged greatly in modern history. (Over geological time, millions of years, there were periods of tropical conditions, making understandable the presence of stored carbon as well as oil and gas deposits).[9] For some parts of the Arctic, there have been eras of warming and cooling. The twentieth century is divided into two periods: two warming periods bracketing an overall cooling period between 1945 and 1966.[10] Recently, the Arctic is deeply cold less often in some places. In northern Russia, mean temperatures in January are almost everywhere below -10°C (14°F), and as low as -45°C (-49°F) in the eastern inland areas. The average annual temperature in Greenland is 8.4°C (47°F). In a region as large and diverse as the Arctic, significant differences exist. Parts of Canada and Greenland surrounding the Labrador Sea have seen cooling in recent years. In the Canadian Arctic, summer temperatures over the last century are the highest they have been in tens of thousands of years.

While often shown in white, precipitation in the Arctic, like temperature, varies. Fairbanks, Alaska, gets about 65 inches of snow (1,651 millimeter) and about 11 inches of rain per year. In Greenland, the average annual rainfall is 1,132 millimeters or about 45 inches. The giant island experiences light snow in the northern and central areas and a bit more south of the Arctic Circle, along the coasts and at high altitudes on the ice sheet.[11] In some parts of the Arctic, including Canada, snowfall can be over 120 inches or about three meters. Many places see considerable fog and are damp.

Different temperatures and amounts of snow and rain are understandable in light of the size of the Arctic—which can be divided into four subregions. East Greenland, northern Scandinavia, northwestern Russia and the Barents Sea constitute region one. The second region is the area from the Urals to Chukotka in Central Siberia, the Barents, Laptev and East Siberian Seas. Region three is Chukotka, Alaska, the western Canadian Arctic to the Mackenzie River and the Bering, Chukchi and Beaufort Seas. Eastern Canada and West Greenland make up the fourth region.[12]

The Arctic Sea first connotes ice; it averages about three meters thick with the thickest sections approximately four to five meters (about 12 to 15 feet). In the summer, parts of the sea are open, increasingly in recent years. Below the ice and water is an ocean floor, a high percentage of which is the continental shelf, that is the edge of the land area that extends underwater. The remainder of the ocean consists of two principal deep basins that are subdivided into four smaller basins. The central part of these ridges extends 1,100 miles (1,770 kilometers) from the continental shelf off Ellesmere Island to the New Siberian Islands—Eastern Siberia to Nunavut Canada. This huge mountain range in the sea was discovered in around 1950. Currents in the ocean influence its climate and diversity. The Arctic has a clockwise movement or drift pattern in the Beaufort Gyre in the western part of the Arctic Ocean. A nearly straight line Transpolar Drift Stream moves eastward across the ocean from the New Siberian Islands to the Fram Strait, between Greenland and Svalbard.

Arctic places are dark continuously in the winter and light in the summer. Above the Arctic Circle, there are 24 hours of daylight in the summer and 24 hours of darkness in the winter. In Alta Norway, there is no daylight at Christmas while there are 24 hours of daylight at the start of Ramadan.

The Arctic is changing, rapidly. Temperatures are rising more than twice as fast as those of the world average; sea ice is receding and thinning; land activities disgorge effluents into the seas. The Arctic is becoming greener (turning from tundra to forest); levels of organic pollutants are rising; species new to the cold North are appearing where not seen before. Indigenous peoples are more influential as their traditional ways of life continue to be threatened. Industry is either watchfully or actively waiting to drill and mine while environmental groups are advocating for greater protection of the natural Arctic. Governments across the globe are working to develop, protect, conserve or exploit resources in this giant place.

How does the changing of the Arctic matter and to whom? Is it of serious concern if the Arctic becomes warmer? If its glaciers shrink away and its polar bears are found in zoos only? Must cultures based on cold be preserved? Is it acceptable if cultures adapt to a less cold world? These questions suggest a larger inquiry: What is a good future of the North? One's conclusion is in one sense personal. But another view is less subjective. What if the Arctic is a canary in the coal mine, or the frog in the pot of water, and what if its warming, thawing, melting and other changes reflect significant global environmental shifts? What if the Arctic's instability affects society as a whole and does not bode well for the future: sunken cities throughout the world, cultural practices precluded, traditions and languages lost, species gone extinct, major metropolitan areas becoming too hot as to be unlivable and massive movements of people from areas becoming deserts or from otherwise inhospitable regions?

Internationally, Arctic nations play major roles in pondering these existential concerns. So it matters which countries are considered Arctic nations. Countries want to be seen as Arctic nations for several reasons. Some have a deep interest in protecting the Arctic: preserving what is pristine and improving what is threatened. Others want access to a potential boom of extractable resources: oil, gas and maybe special metals. And some want to influence major international transit routes and rules for going through them to save time and money for international trade. At times, nations see international security and military advantages associated with being Arctic. Who has and should have the decision-making power is a matter of high global stakes. If a country is classified as "Arctic," it will argue that it should have a strong voice in decision making regarding what happens in and to the region.

The powerful European Union (EU) views the Arctic as important for many reasons. National security, environmental protection, concern with indigenous peoples, different views on whaling and other traditional practices motivate the EU. More directly, it obtains over 40 percent of its oil and almost 60 percent of its natural gas from Norway and Russia. It helps in sorting out the EU's interests that it is a political and economic union of 27 member states. It is not itself a member of certain important Arctic organizations, but some of its member states are. It is both an intergovernmental and supranational organization—a unique international institution. Not all of its members share views on sustainability questions, and a few have direct influence in major Arctic organizations.

It is not just the Arctic Eight and Europe which want a place at the table. China calls itself a "near Arctic state," and India, Singapore, Vietnam and Korea also seek Arctic voices. In 2018, China announced to the world its position on the region in a white paper on the Arctic with images of a Polar Silk Road. The policy laid out goals of resource extraction, scientific study and preserving the region's environment; it hopes to create an Arctic Blue Economic Corridor. China is already a formal observer in international Arctic organizations and has made some important investments. The Russian Arctic is a particular focus; it is close to some parts of China. As the relations between China and Russia become increasingly warm, there are fewer obstacles to Russian trade and tourism travel. Non-Arctic countries clamor to enter into Arctic international organizations and to create new ones. Countries look to the North with plans for investment, trade and resource extraction while seeking to develop allies and soft power. Some aim just to have their citizens enjoy the region.

The Arctic is important well beyond its place. It is important to people in Miami and Bangladesh and Italy and California and Australia. What happens in the Far North dramatically affects the world. The function of the Arctic in sea-level rise—a major global concern—is significant. In 2018, the global sea level was 3.2 inches (81.3 millimeter) above the 1993 average—the highest annual average in the satellite record (1993–present). The average rate of sea level rise is accelerating. Scientists are very confident that global mean sea level will rise at least eight inches (203 millimeter) and up to 6.6 feet (over 2,000 millimeter) by 2100, depending on the energy decisions we make.[13] In the United States, almost 40 percent of the population lives in relatively densely populated coastal areas where the sea level plays a role in flooding, shoreline erosion and hazards from storms. Globally, 8 percent of the world's largest cities are near a coast, according to the UN Atlas of the Oceans.

And the 99.95 percent of people who do not live in the Arctic must know that the Arctic is important to those who live there in an existential sense. Arctic people, and cultures, and nature matter simply because they *are*. Non-Arctic people affect the lives of millions of permanent Arctic inhabitants in many ways. Global flows go in both directions. Some atmospheric pollution in the Arctic comes from Europe in the form of black carbon and as other toxic pollutants from many other countries. Certain toxic substances get into the food stuffs of Arctic people. And the "hole" in the ozone that exposes Arctic residents to radiation is a result of activities of countries from all over the world. Climate change, caused by almost all of humanity, has particularly marked consequences for the Arctic and its peoples, because of which temperatures in Arctic regions have reached unprecedented high levels. In some Arctic places, snow has changed to rain. Erosion of seacoasts is commonplace. There are more wildfires. The ocean is becoming more acidic. Permafrost is no longer permanent.

Changes do not come only from climate shifts. Businesses and institutions make their marks in other ways. Industries use timber throughout the world disrupting the biological resources of the region. The habitats of wildlife which sustain many of the Arctic people are hence altered. Caribou and reindeer are injured in new ways by resource extraction and energy production practices, their migration patterns shifted their predators become more common. Arctic peoples' diets are disrupted, and traditional activities such as hunting and herding are threatened. Vessels passing through the sea dump or offload pollutants—intentionally or by accident. Other ships carrying tourists to the Arctic, despite bringing in resources that can be beneficial, also pollute and damage cultural sites and traditions. And some laws made outside of the Arctic prohibit Arctic people from practices they have engaged in for centuries.

What can society do about these global changes cycling to and from the Arctic? To be sure, what happens in the North depends in part on natural forces that are beyond how people treat it. But conditions in the Arctic now and in the future also depend on how people interact with it.

Many strategies exist to protect, improve and manage the region, and many others are offered. They come from several places. A remarkably large number of laws and policies targets conditions in the Arctic. Rules emanate from state and local governments, indigenous groups as well as regional and international bodies. In education, new lessons are being more widely taught about the people, environment and histories of the region. Educators also point to what more can be done. Foundations and other philanthropists give to sustain the Arctic—these include funding activities from managing national parks to supporting native peoples in governing their home places. Governments are increasingly focusing on the region, creating agencies and research units to study the Arctic, funding programs for indigenous peoples and for infrastructure development, for environmental protection, economic development and for security. And through a panoply of organizations and groups, what has come to be known as civil society drives to an ever-greater extent what formal institutions decide about and how they act in the Arctic.

Does this array of actions come together for a positive future for the Arctic? The answer depends on what the goal for the Arctic is. It may be that water quality, air quality as well as the health of plants, animals and other organisms are maintained, or improved, or allowed to degrade an acceptable amount as a tradeoff for economic growth. Or a main objective might be to support sustainable traditional lifestyles and improve living conditions. Or hopes may be more modest: that environmental targets are met; that countries cooperate to fight pollution; that new laws and policies are adopted; that education about the oceans is deepened; and that millennia-old traditions are supported.

THIS BOOK

Polar Shift is about the future of the Arctic with concern for all of these goals. But first, in Chapter 2, we introduce the Arctic: how it has been understood historically, how people imagine it, its present boundaries and social conditions. We lay out how it has been portrayed in literature and art and when and how it was explored. We then see it now: its tundra and permafrost, its shopping malls, big cities and remote villages; its glaciers; its dirt roads, streets and highways; its fishing and whaling unions; and its people carving sculptures, hunting and attending its schools and universities. We note the great commonalities and the gaping differences among areas and peoples within the Arctic.

To know whether the way the Arctic is managed is sustainable, we need to know the conditions of the Arctic and how they are changing. In Chapter 3, we learn, perhaps not surprisingly, that although some of these conditions are known, there are many gaps in knowledge. That said, much is understood about pollution there, both air and water. We know how and how fast climate is changing. We understand, quite well, the status of Arctic marine life, the environmental conditions on land and the degradation of that land. We know about the status of the flora and fauna of the region. And we know somewhat about the health and standard of living of its peoples.

Chapter 4 describes how the Arctic is managed. We present the great range of law, policy and social action targeting environmental quality and sustainability of the region. We explain the rules—whether they be indigenous, local, national, regional or international. Who rules and how in villages, cities, counties, provinces, states, oblasts and in places where the rules are not defined by political boundaries? We chronicle that at times well-motivated people are at loggerheads—seeking different goals with different understandings of what it means to be sustaining—about what is important to a good future Arctic. We ask, are the rules and efforts enough? In Chapter 5, we address what should be done where they are not, evaluating recommendations for sustaining and improving this global resource of incalculable value.

A WORD ON METHODS

How does one address a topic as important and complex as Arctic sustainability? With modesty. Summaries and conclusions in this book represent my best attempts to take the most current and respected work on the Arctic and make it accessible to the interested citizen who cares about the region and to specialists about fields that are new to them. I hope this work reflects the overall conclusions of researchers in specific areas—glaciology, anthropology, indigenous studies, demographics, earth system science, environmental science, law and so on—well.

Polar Shift echoes my own work as well as summarizes, synthesizes and incorporates materials from leading Arctic experts. As recorded in the endnotes, the sections on conditions in the Arctic, Chapter 3, reflect ongoing assessments of the leading reports from national and international scientific groups. This analysis, interpretation and communication has been an ongoing project of mine for decades and is updated on a regular basis. Similarly, Chapter 2's description of the Arctic as a place, historically and now, is based on leading government reports, scholarly analyses from history and literature, the social sciences, international relations, anthropology and sociology as well as highly credible think tanks, nongovernmental organizations and journalistic sources. The review of Arctic sustainability law and governance, Chapters 4 and 5, is original. It is based on many sources: legal research, a survey of hundreds of Arctic experts,[14] interviews of people in each of the Arctic places (of government officials at all levels, indigenous leaders, fishers and hunters, researchers and other workers in the Arctic); on university-sponsored policy workshops on Arctic governance; on attending, presenting and listening at a large number of meetings on Arctic sustainability; and on site stays in all of the Arctic regions[15] Across all fields, I have benefited also from social media and from monitoring, on a daily basis, educated commentary on the remarkable story of life in the region and changes in it.

NOTES

1 Throughout, I mainly use the term indigenous. Where appropriate, I employ native or aboriginal. The histories and politics of first peoples (preinvasion or precolonial societies) are complex. I attempt to use the terms that they and the documents which describe them employ.

2 Kim Rutledge et al., "Permafrost," National Geographic, last updated Feb. 15, 2011, accessed February 7, 2022,https://www.nationalgeographic.org/encyclopedia/permafrost/.

3 "Percent Forest Cover in the Boreal Forest Biome (2000)," Data Basin, accessed February 7, 2022, https://databasin.org/maps/new/#datasets=d842914b159244e8829677eaf5ea62eb.

4 Gunter Weller, "Summary and Synthesis of the ACIA," in *Arctic Climate Impact Assessment*, ed. Carolyn Simon (New York: Cambridge University Press, 2005), 1002.

5 The north magnetic pole has been slowly moving across the Canadian Arctic toward Russia for many years. Since its discovery in 1831, the pole has traveled 1,400 miles. The magnetic field reverses its polarity every several 100,000 years. Ashley Strickland, "Earth's Magnetic North Pole Is Heading for Russia for Russia and Scientists are Puzzled," December 18, 2019, accessed September 9, 2020, https://edition.cnn.com/2019/12/18/world/magnetic-north-pole-drift-scn-trnd/index.html.

6 Audrey Ramming, "Russian Navy Confirms Emergence of Five New Islands in the Arctic Ocean," GlacierHub, November 21, 2019, accessed September 6, 2020, https://glacierhub.org/2019/11/21/russian-navy-confirms-emergence-of-five-new-islands-in-the-arctic-ocean/.

7 Naomi Friedman, "Our Interconnected Ocean," National Geographic, accessed February 7, 2022, https://www.nationalgeographic.org/activity/our-interconnected-ocean/. Recently some have been identifying the waters around Antarctica as the Southern Ocean. "How Many Oceans Are There?," National Ocean Service, June 8, 2021, accessed June 18, 2021, https://oceanservice.noaa.gov/facts/howmanyoceans.html.

8 "How Close Is Alaska to Russia?," Alaska Public Lands Information Centers, accessed August 6, 2019, https://www.alaskacenters.gov/visitors-centers/faqs/how-close-alaska-russia.

9 "Arctic Climate History," USGS, accessed August 4, 2021, https://geology.er.usgs.gov/egpsc/arcticpaleoceanography/arcticclimatehistory.html. My thanks to an anonymous reviewer for reminding me to make this point.

10 Weller, "Summary and Synthesis of the ACIA," 992.

11 "Climate—Greenland," Climates to Travel, World Climate Guide, https://www.climatestotravel.com/climate/greenland.

12 Weller, "Summary and Synthesis of the ACIA," 1003.

13 Aria Bendix, "Amazon Is Headed to Long Island City, Queens—An Area That Could Be Underwater by 2100," Business Insider, November, 13, 2018, accessed February 7, 2022, https://www.businessinsider.com/amazon-hq2-long-island-city-underwater-2018-11.

14 The survey (UCI Arctic Expert Survey) solicited the views of experts on Arctic governance with a focus on analyses that can advance policy consideration and promote a sustainable Arctic. We use results and comments throughout based from the general

trends in expert answers. Because of the nature of the responding group, no statistical significance is attributed to quantitative results. We used judgment sampling (or purposive sampling). This is a common nonprobability method of obtaining a sample based on an assessment of what best represents the population of interest. Judgment sampling requires expert knowledge of the specific subject matter.

The population of individuals with sufficient knowledge to answer the questions proposed in the survey was created using a combination of approaches. We first compiled a list of all government officials at the federal level in 21 countries; these are people whose work is relevant to oceans and Arctic policy within state or foreign affairs agencies, as well as within any separate agency that contained a special focus on the oceans, such as the National Oceanic and Atmospheric Administration. The countries were Canada, the United States, Russia, Finland, Norway, Iceland, Sweden, Denmark, France, Germany, the Italian Republic, Japan, the Netherlands, the People's Republic of China, Poland, the Republic of India, the Republic of Korea, the Republic of Singapore, Spain, Switzerland and the UK. We then extracted contact information for agencies where available.

The second parallel round of sample selection involved identifying organizations—indigenous, governmental and nongovernmental—with foci on the Arctic Ocean or land regions, irrespective of organization size. We also selected research units within universities and individuals whose specific research interests fit within Arctic environmental governance or sustainability. In addition, we identified potential survey respondents through searches of relevant Arctic-related publications (the authors) and conference programs and presentations on relevant topics. Some of these were identified through our direct participation in Arctic programs and through travels to Arctic regions. There we also interviewed policymakers, scientists, indigenous peoples and academics.

We incorporated helpful suggestions on the survey instrument related to communication, clarity and the probability of a response. After our pretests of the survey, we invited contacts to participate in it online and to suggest names of people who may have interest in the subject matter of the survey.

The survey was administered through the University of California's eee survey system. It opened for response on August 29, 2018; results here reflect comments through late October 2019. Of the 1,440 requests that were sent, we received 220 completed responses.

To maximize participation, we sent individually addressed email letters to contacts: once for the initial contact and a second time as a reminder within one to three weeks from the initial contact question.

15 See "Environmental Governance and Management in the Arctic," *U.C. Irvine Sch. L. Ctr. Land, Env't, & Nat. Res.* (April 21–22, 2016); "Advancing Ecosystem-Based Marine Management in the Arctic: Recommendations to the Arctic Council Task Force on Arctic Marine Cooperation by the UC Irvine School of Law Center for Land, Environment, and Natural Resources (CLEANR)," https://www.law.uci.edu/centers/cleanr/events/workshops.html; "Legal Strategies to Address Climate Change in the North American Arctic," *U.C. Irvine Sch. L. Ctr. Land, Env't, & Nat. Res.* (October 27–28, 2017); and "Arctic Governance, Marine Ecosystem Protection in the Arctic," June 18, 2021, Scoping session, https://www.law.uci.edu/centers/cleanr/events/workshops.html.

2

THE PLACE: IN HISTORY AND NOW

Outside Nunavut, the Canadian official was in an area where thousands of caribou roam. He set up his tripod. An old man with a cane hobbled by, sighted the tripod and cried with happiness at being able to hunt again although that day he did not snag an animal.[1]

Koovian[2] drives me in her gray Toyota Tundra to Jerry's mother's house, where he creates his art in a work shed. His brother greeted Jerry from the porch located near this large wooden structure.[3] Jerry's work, which involves making beautiful art pieces with soapstone, marble, glass, ivory, antler, wood and granite, is too noisy and dusty to carry out at his own apartment complex. He chops, grinds, saws into and then sands the limestone, creating polished gray and black marine mammals, *quilliq* (Inuit oil lamps) and iconic images of Nunavut. He also makes harpoon spearheads for the bowhead hunt—one was scheduled three weeks after our visit. These weapons are like giant jewels, large as a man's hand, smooth and golden.

Jerry had agreed to introduce me to his homeland. He suggests we talk in his car, a black older model parked near his work shed. So we drive together to the nearby high school as he wants to show me all the things he was going to talk about.

There is a housing crisis; we look out over to a mid-sized home, wooden, a bit tired but with views of Frobisher Bay, listed for $800,000. We survey the bay whose ice surface had changed this year. Hunting is now dangerous. Even the elders, experienced hunters, cannot gauge the thickness of the ice and some of their snowmobiles and all their hunting supplies have crashed through it.

The climate is changing. I ask, "Do you think the changes are caused by us, by people?" "Some do, I don't," Jerry says. "Changes occur over long periods of time and this is one." People see that there are now different birds; there are more insects. The fog is more pronounced, more rain fall and there is more flooding. "Houses collapse." But people don't agree on what's caused the change and how to adapt to it.

We talk about the new airport, which was a great surprise to me when my First Air jet touched down from Ottawa. It still has the smell of newly completed construction, its walls covered with rich cloth hangings in deep colors of purple and red that were exhibited along with art pieces of the Nunavut Territory, like Jerry's. Many were on sale—some for over a $1,000—near a pizza counter. Some parts of the road to the airport were paved a couple of days before, and appeared black and smooth, whereas the rest of the route to the center of town was still dirt and gravel. Jerry thinks that the expense for the new airport facility was wasted. "Could have used the money for other things, housing for example," he says in English. He bemoans the fact that the young Inuit are not learning the language well with the school's focus on immersion in Inuktitut in the early grades. The young will need to speak English better than they currently do if they are to move into jobs being created in the North. "Could have altered the airline schedules instead. The old airport was crowded only twice every day." The two airlines, First Air and Canadian North, fly the same schedule, to the same place at exactly the same time every day (13:15 hours). "Charge them for the rights and alternate the days on which they have a more attractive departure schedule."

Across the street from the spanking new airport is a long three- or four-story building in green. It looks as if it could be a site for the ubiquitous Airport Marriott or Holiday Inn or Hilton. However, this building is a molding, asbestos-filled deserted environmental mess. It had once served as a barracks or a hotel for the American military. It was then used—depending on whose story one believes—to house Inuit children from across Nunavut to live "in residence" to attend school and learn Canadian languages.[4] Just behind the "non-Hilton" is a jail. Although it looks like a black heavy plastic modular structure, it is secure—so secure that inmates had complained of the conditions and rioted just days before my arrival in Iqaluit. Many were then charged for threatening the guards or throwing food. Some men and older boys were later transferred by air by the Royal Canadian Mounted Police (RCMP), the sheriff and other correctional officers to Ottawa where they would be imprisoned with more seasoned criminals and gang members. The trip for many of the boys was their first time on a plane—the first time they would see a tree, the first time they would be without their Inuit families. They were afraid and some were crying.

A couple blocks away is the imposing and famous igloo-shaped Anglican church. Many Inuit are Anglican or Catholic. The few modern buildings in town are dome-like, including the elementary school which resembles the Broad Museum in Los Angeles having a white, geometric and pocked facade. I am told it was supposed to look like a whale blubber.

Later, Koovian offers to show me around after dinner. Now we drive in her truck in the evening mid-day light. We pass a simple but comfortable looking housing complex near the beach and she tells me that the Inuit elders live in these units. At some point, the older Inuit leave their family homes and come here, a place that is much different from where they were born—usually in tents or in igloos depending on the time of the year. "Eskimos are born in igloos": this depiction is not pejorative. Koovian notes, "That's what we say." The elders from the complex and elders from the community meet together every day to have their afternoon tea and talk and visit. They have caretakers who help them. They enjoy the times local children stop by to visit.

We take a tour of a national park situated near Iqaluit. The park is wind-blown, has low vegetation, is on the water, and there are places where campers have set up their tents. The larger canvas ones are those of the Inuit; the others, REI style, belong to the visitors. Some of the national parks in the territory are gigantic and lie empty; one such camp gets only 70 visitors a year.

The beauty of the park near Iqaluit is like that of Iceland, both desolate and welcoming, empty yet filled with warmth. But one of the entrances is near a giant, hideous dump, which is where the *Crystal Serenity* docked during its maiden cruise passage in 2016. As we drive in and through it, we find its fences ripped, with all sorts of debris spewed around—some not so bad, like bailed cardboard; others unidentifiable—next to abandoned cars, trailers and tires. Plastic blows to and from a nearby site where huskies, dozens of them, are tied next to sheds.

"I would have let it burn," said the mayor about the landfill, as we talked in her modest office in town. She was not the mayor when the fire that lasted for months began. It took $45 million of the budget to finally extinguish the putrid blaze: "Better to have let it burn and to make a statement." Soon this site will be covered and a large new dump built, upwind, in another area of pristine rock and low-lying vegetation located in the hill above town.

"Kill the myth of the Arctic," Mary Ellen, the head of research at Arctic University, pleads as we talk; she is sitting in her wheelchair on top of the remarkable floor map of the Arctic as big as a good-sized circular conference room. She asks to get rid of the romanticism of the beautiful polar bear and the whale, of the mythology and of the natives in seal skins. She says the vast majority of Canadians know nothing about Nunavut, asking her colleagues: "What currency do you use up there?"

On the topic of Canadian rules for the territories, Ellen is critical of the priorities of research funding for protecting the Arctic. Research stations are sited unfortunately for reasons of politics and security, and not to create realistic chances of attracting good and committed scientists willing to work in remote areas for sustained periods.

The Arctic and its future are our subjects. What is the Arctic? No one can claim a superior answer to this question. But there are many ways of getting a satisfying sense of the Arctic, both for those who live there and those who do not. Looking to history and art helps; how has the Arctic been envisioned over the centuries? Describing territories that are generally said to be in the Arctic is another topic that needs further examination. Meeting its peoples is central to knowing the Arctic; these peoples live in places that are defined as Arctic countries by various indicators where the boundaries of countries are irrelevant. How are these people similar, say like Europeans or Africans are similar? How do they differ? To understand better how to sustain the Arctic, it helps to know them, and it is essential to appreciate how the environment, both social and physical, in which they live is changing.

Images of what the Arctic is and represents have deep historical antecedents. Over the centuries, the Arctic has been envisioned in many ways: sometimes fictional, sometimes exotic, sometimes bizarre—often romanticized. To many, the Arctic was what the world came to know or imagine about as a very remote place through art. Readers or museumgoers saw pictures depicting native people—often benign and content, dressed in simple garb or in clothes that overpower the physique with their hides and pelts. With ruddy complexions, their faces ensconced in hooded fur, they gather and sit in wood and skin dwellings, or sometimes in communal huts, at the center of which a fire warms them. They await their fish, frying in melted grease. Through paintings and reproductions, those interested in the Arctic viewed the Sámi encampments with these nomads in their colorful dress, near their *lavvu* (tents, like tipi) or long houses. Alternately, the subjects portrayed were working people, making their way, always in silence it seemed, across the tundra in their sledges or sleds. There were dogs frolicking in the snow in Eastern Siberia. Then a sailing ship moving into a protected, untouched bay in Norway, mountains rising from the shore permanently covered with pristine white snow. Or the dogs pulling a sledge or *narta*, across the landscape against a blinding white background, and yet the backgrounds were all different.[5] Peaceful figures dominated, the exceptions being an intense face of a shaman in his flowing garb or a child in fear as a visiting puritanical preacher tries shame to rid her parents of their indigenous ways.

There were many boats in these pictures: for exploring, for sailing in the open sea or just for fishing. Their prows are turned up, and with the shapes of their sterns and their wide hulls, they resemble ancient Viking ships.

The Group of Seven, a group of famous Canadian landscape painters, portrayed a lifeless mammoth frozen land. The work of Lawren Harris, a member of this group, offered bold scenes of snow and ice forms in abstract and stark white light. Other art schools saw the Arctic as God's temple, "The City of God! The sea of glass! The plains of heaven!" or as "beyond man's footprints," a "dreary waste of grey, verily a region still unmastered by human skill and courage." Pictured was a place of the "ever present danger of sudden or lingering death." Polar bears, then and now, were a central focus: sometimes they were the victims, while other scenes had them devouring explorers who in some depictions devoured each other, desperate in the merciless ice.[6]

In the minds of some, based on newspapers and rumors, the Arctic would bring vast wealth to men and women strong enough to enter the frontier. Gold had been found in Klondike in the 1870s and in Alaska in 1896. In the Gold Rush, 10,000 hopeful people, many called stampeders, left their homes in the Canadian Yukon and Alaska to undertake a treacherous and often tragic trek, disastrous for them and also for some native peoples as well as for the waters, the forests and the land. The adventurous trudged slowly across ice valleys and at times through unpassable clogged and slippery terrain—one such place was the Dead Horse Trail, named so after 3,000 horses died while traversing through it.

The Arctic, although forbidding, also attracted people for reasons other than wealth. Explorers sought new routes, not only for trade and gold, but for adventure. Traveling north from Europe to East Asia was a goal or at least an ideal for hundreds of years. Some date the notion back to Ptolemy.[7] Northwest Passage expeditions—dreamed of, and carried out—were numerous. Mostly they failed. In 1497, a Venetian navigator living in England became the first European to explore the Northwest Passage. Sailing from Bristol, England, John Cabot (Giovanni Caboto) thought he had reached the shores of Asia but got as far as what are now known as the maritime, eastern, provinces of Canada. The next year, he undertook a second larger expedition. His ships and crew never returned, probably shipwrecked in the North Atlantic. In 1534, the French sent Jacques Cartier to seek a faster route to Asia. He and his crew of 61 men reached what is now Newfoundland and the Gulf of St. Lawrence but not the Northwest Passage. Cartier undertook two more trips, one making its way to the area of the city he is credited with founding: Quebec. An unsuccessful third voyage was undertaken in 1541.

Leaving from a different continent, in 1539, Spanish explorer Francisco de Ulloa left Acapulco, Mexico, searching for a Pacific route to the Northwest Passage. He sailed as far as the Gulf of California, or the Sea of Cortés, unable to find a strait that he thought could take him Far North. In 1609, Henry Hudson traveled for the Dutch East India Company to find the Northwest Passage from the Atlantic to the Pacific. Hudson first sailed around Long Island and into New York's Hudson River, but turned back having discovered no channel to the Far North. His second try was tragic. Attempting the journey through the Hudson Bay, he and his crew were trapped by the ice; the crew mutinied, set Hudson adrift and he disappeared forever.

Similarly tragic was the attempt in 1845 of English Royal Navy officer and Arctic explorer Sir John Franklin. Franklin's expedition set sail with 128 men aboard two ships, the HMS *Erebus* and the aptly named HMS *Terror*. The ships vanished. It is suspected that both vessels became ice-bound and were abandoned by their crews. Five years later, the Irish explorer Robert McClure left from England in search of the Franklin disaster. In this attempt, McClure became the first person to traverse the Northwest Passage; he did so partially by sea and partially by sled over ice. Fifty years later in 1906, the larger dream was realized when Roald Amundsen, a Norwegian explorer, would make the entire passage by sea.

These were explorers dreaming but sometimes rationally planning, and their exploits made for great public interest.

Other images of the Arctic were among the most frightening of the reading public, including young people growing up with exciting literature:

> "But soon," he cried with sad and solemn enthusiasm, "I shall die, and what I now feel be no longer felt. Soon these burning miseries will be extinct. I shall ascend my funeral pile triumphantly and exult in the agony of the torturing flames [...] my ashes will be swept into the sea by the winds."
>
> He sprang from the cabin-window as he said this, upon the ice raft which lay close to the vessel. He was soon borne away by the waves and lost in darkness and distance. He was the Monster; the sea was the Arctic.[8] He had come to his creator, Victor Frankenstein. The Monster had pledged to incinerate himself at "the Northernmost extremity of the globe."[9]

Other literary depictions of the Arctic speak of a Black Rectangle Labelled "Polar Night"; of the "City of the Sun on Ice"; of men, mysteries and monsters.[10] It is a "place at the edge of, or beyond, culture"; a place of extremes—of gulags, of nuclear submarines deep in a frigid sea, and of people trying the extraordinary—or journeys to get to the North Pole by a hydrogen balloon, of canines called by the wild, of journeys to bleak cold places, of female self-discovery.[11]

The surrealistic visions and understandings of the Arctic extend into technically challenging and even disturbing territory. Joscelyn Godwin's work *ARKTOS, The Polar Myth in Science, Symbolism, and Nazi Survival* summarizes how writers have perceived the Arctic or the Pole or the North differently.[12] If the earth did not tilt at an awkward angle from the perpendicular, if it sat erect in its orbit around the sun, on one of the continents that would then exist would appear "the second Race, of monstrous, androgynous, semi-human beings [...] the first attempt of material nature at building human bodies." They perished "in the first great cataclysm, as Greenland and the other northern 'Eden with their eternal spring' were transformed into hyperborean Hades."

Godwin writes about Jules Verne's *The Purchase of the Pole* as a warning against technocratic arrogance, perhaps a harbinger of thoughts on geoengineering strategies to save the Arctic today. Verne's book is about a consortium that buys up enormous areas of Arctic regions very cheaply because they are thought to be worthless. The cunning speculators then install a gigantic cannon on Mount Kilimanjaro (Tanzania) intending "to push the earth sufficiently off its axial tilt to bring polar regions within a temperate zone, thus making them inestimably valuable."[13]

Then there are the persistent stories of the Arctic's links to a Nazi quest for a superior race. Years after World War II, Russian scientists discovered a secret base in the Arctic on Alexandra Land. According to one story, Hitler ordered its construction in 1942. The Russians found items with the Nazi symbol. Might the expedition have been part of the work of or for Ahnenerb, a Nazi Germany institute that undertook research on the Aryan race, trying to prove that mythological Nordic populations once ruled the world?[14] People belonging to the Aryan race were biologically distinct: tall and blond. Hitler and some Nazis espoused the notion that Aryans were responsible for all significant developments in human culture. In *Mein Kampf*, Hitler wrote:

> It was not by mere chance that the first forms of civilization arose there where the Aryan came into contact with inferior races, subjugated them and forced them to obey his command [...] By imposing on them a useful, though hard, manner of employing their powers he not only spared the lives of those whom he had conquered but probably made their lives easier than these had been in the former state of so-called "freedom." While he ruthlessly maintained his position as their master, he not only remained master but he also maintained and advanced civilization. For this depended exclusively on his inborn abilities and, therefore, on the preservation of the Aryan race as such.[15]

Americans also formed contrasting views of Arctic people. Samuel George Morton, a famous American craniologist and theorist on multiple racial creations, described the "Polar Family." He portrayed Arctic

> people to be, both in appearance and in manner, among the most repulsive of the human species [...] crafty, sensual, ungrateful, obstinate and unfeeling [...] Their mental faculties from infancy to old age present a continued childhood; they reach a certain limit and expand no further [...] In gluttony, selfishness and ingratitude, they are perhaps unequaled by any other nation of people.[16]

But Elisha Kent Kane, inspired during the American Civil War by news of Arctic expeditions, gathered men from throughout the Union to set off "to a seascape remote from sectional antagonism and free of the divisive enticements of conquest, extraction, and development."[17] Henry Clay agreed with this search and became the principal and crucial supporter of congressional backing for the Arctic voyages.[18]

Official US interests in the Arctic have ebbed and flowed. In 1867, the United States purchased Alaska for $7.2 million—not, it turned out, a "Seward's Folly." Later, in 1946, it attempted to buy Greenland for $100 million. Then in 2019, President Trump asked his advisors about a second attempt at purchasing the giant island. Neither Greenland nor Denmark wanted a deal. In general, the United States has been a reluctant Arctic actor. As one historian summarized: "The Arctic has remained persistently outside the realm of U.S. conceptions of national identity, security, and history. At discrete moments, it has provided a stage on which Americans can perform some idea, extract some victory, distract from some anxiety. But it has always been another space, exoticized and exploited to different ends, then departed and ignored."[19]

Today for many—not its inhabitants—the Arctic is still a mysterious place—or an unknown. It is "one of the Poles," not the one with sweet giant penguins. It is remote, dark, but with the midnight sun. It is home to whales considered benign wondrous creatures, and polar bears considered by non-Arctic people as gentle and even cuddly. Eskimos live there in snow and a lot of ice.[20] The Arctic is where Santa lives: the cold, beautifully snowy place where happy people make wonderful toys to be shipped out on Christmas Eve—out of the Arctic, but not on its seas—through the air.

Santa's home holds a special place in the minds of many Western children and their parents. Europeans to this day take expensive vacations in the cold dark of the Arctic winter. An Italian site offers a "Viaggio al Polo Nord con i bambini": "Travel to the North Pole with the children for an unforgettable vacation for the whole family and realize a dream for the little ones and the old [...] a trip [...] that all children and adults dream of and should do at least once in their life, if only to meet Santa in person."[21]

In the aggregate, these notions present a mixed perception: The Arctic as a mammoth, pristine, environmentally preserved, heavenly yet threatening place.

THE ARCTIC TODAY

What is factual about the Arctic? Who are its people? Where do they live? How are they different from each other? How is their place, their environment, changing? What do they share? As to characteristics that are shared by Arctic people, a distinction sometimes made between, on the one hand, United States, Greenland and Canada and, on the other, the European Arctic, highlights some indicators. (Russia is both European and Asian in territory but more European in population.) Food insecurity, health status and other social indicators vary owing to this dichotomy with generally higher standards of living in the European sector, although there are many exceptions to this simple division. Arctic people have more differences among them than what they have in common.

But some characteristics, individual and societal, are shared:

> There is nothing akin to having been born in the Arctic. Childhood is spent surrounded by Arctic dwellers who are grateful for the honour of being one with the strong winds, the mighty rivers and the ocean which shapes their lives. The imaginations of indigenous children are lifted to new heights as they listen to stories that pay homage to Arctic natural wonders.[22]

Most centrally, Arctic places share the Arctic Ocean, and the Arctic people not only benefit from resources and services the ocean provides but are also impacted by it. Most practically, nations that self-identify as Arctic all belong to Arctic governmental, quasigovernmental and nongovernmental organizations. Each Arctic country (except for Iceland) is home to indigenous peoples and has been for thousands of years. Most of these people lived traditionally, hunting, fishing, herding and gathering plants for food. Crossing what are now defined as country boundaries or within them are the Sámi in circumpolar areas of Finland, Sweden, Norway and northwest Russia; the Nenets, Khanty, Evenk and Chukchi in Russia; Aleut, Yupik and Inuit (Iñupiat) in Alaska; Inuit (Inuvialuit) in Canada; and Inuit (Kalaallit) in Greenland—in all they comprise about 40 ethnic groups.[23] Tragically, the Arctic also shares, to a great extent, the treatment meted out by majoritarian or colonizing peoples as there exists a history of disrespect, domination and abuse of many native peoples.

All Arctic nations now have people who arrived here later than those who historically inhabited the area, namely, the settlers—that is the Greenlanders, Danes, Icelanders, Swedes, Norwegians, Finns, Russians, Canadians and Americans. The newer residents are the hyphenated Arctic people throughout the North: Chinese-Norwegians, Filipino-Canadians, Italian-Icelanders, Iraqi-Swedes and recently, as a result of a refugee crisis, Syrian-Norwegians.

Some animals are distinctively Arctic: the caribou, the narwhal, wolves, polar bears, some species of whale, reindeer—this last, sustenance and a sacred presence. In the language of Northern Sámi in parts of Finland, Sweden and Norway, a herd of reindeer is called *Ealiu*. Each animal within a herd is described by herders—with up to 500 words—who distinguish each member of the herd by its unique characteristic, from temperament of the animal to the pattern of antlers.[24]

Common across boundaries are certain social characteristics. Leading Arctic organizations are now working to create useful social indicators for the Arctic peoples. This is not an easy task because of lack of information in some subareas, differing views of what constitutes successful and desirable human development, and because of differing ideas of which groups should be compared.[25] Yet much is known. The life expectancy of Arctic peoples, those who live in the Arctic parts of Arctic nations, in 2012–16 was 74.7 years. This compares with an average for the Arctic countries themselves of about 82 years. Russia is an exception at about 73 years. While education levels are high in the nations that make up the Arctic, this is not the case for some of the Arctic parts of those countries. In remote areas, many students do not complete upper secondary school, and there are self-reported functional difficulties at school, home and in leisure activities. Some of these are linked to mental health problems. Also relevant is the nature of jobs and the economy in parts of the Arctic. Boys in more rural areas have options available because of their backgrounds: for example, traditional work such as herding reindeer.

There are some shared patterns of mental health. Arctic regions of the United States, Canada and Russia have considerably higher suicide rates than those of the non-Arctic regions of those countries. In Canada, indigenous communities have suicide rates higher than those of the general Canadian population.[26] For the Inuit, rates rank among the world's highest. In one study period (1999–2003), suicides in Inuit regions averaged 135 per 100,000; over 10 times that of Canada in general.[27] The Inuit situation has gotten considerably worse in recent years, due in major part to the dramatic increase in the number of younger people committing suicide.[28] Suicide rates in some Arctic regions are the highest among teenagers, and young women are more often the victims in Canada. Why these rates are found in the Arctic is not fully understood, but they have been the source of both speculation and social science research. Suicide in the Arctic is linked with and to the loss of cultural continuity and consumption of large quantities of alcohol.

In many Arctic places, the high price of food and the changes in diets of indigenous peoples have made for the phenomenon now called food insecurity: people, and especially children, do not have adequate nutrition.[29] The costs of feeding a family in Inuit Canada, for example, are much higher than a shopping cart of the same foods in Ottawa.[30] This is a phenomenon within an Arctic nation, and it is noted also in Russia; hence it is not everywhere that a European status is central to describing differences among Arctic peoples.[31]

ECONOMIES

Fish play a central role in Arctic economies. Fisheries represent about 90 percent of the export earnings of Greenland, 33 percent in Iceland and about 6 percent in Norway. In the large Arctic states of Russia and the United States, which have more diversified and larger economies, fish sales comprise about 1 percent of the export earnings. The Arctic is rich in some natural resources, and there are many such reserves throughout the whole North. In 2003, natural resource exploitation accounted for about 31 percent of Arctic gross domestic product (GDP) with even higher levels in Russian and North American areas and contributed 5 to 10 percent of the workforce in the European Arctic. About 25 percent of the world's natural gas and 10 percent of oil are produced in the Arctic. According to a 2008 estimate, undiscovered/untapped resources could amount to 90 billion barrels of oil, 50 trillion cubic meters of natural gas and 44 billion barrels of natural gas liquids. Thirteen percent of the world's undiscovered, technically recoverable, oil and up to 30 percent of its gas are estimated to be in the Arctic, while approximately 84 percent of it is offshore. Most of the region's oil reserves are in Alaska, whereas natural gas more than oil is concentrated in Russia's seas. Exploitation in the seas remains a frontier, but onshore oil and gas have been produced for decades.[32]

In many other ways the Arctic is not homogenous. Called by some of its inhabitants as nations or countries, the various places that comprise the land are distinctive. In the following sections, starting from Greenland and going east, we introduce, by country, the lands and waters as well as the Arctic peoples—the settlers and the indigenous.

Greenland / Denmark

All of Greenland is Arctic as defined by latitude, and it fits all of the other criteria (member of Arctic international organizations, year around average temperatures, etc.). The biggest island in the world, Greenland, is the least populated of the Arctic nations. It has roughly 60,000 people in an area about one-fifth the size of the United States. Nuuk, the capital, accounts for just under a third of the total population of Greenland, whose majority ethnic group is Inuit. The Inuit are indigenous peoples who also live in Alaska, Canada and Siberia. The Inuit have survived in Greenland where others have failed.

Greenland is not a fully independent nation. It gained status as a county of Denmark in 1953 and earned Home Rule in 1979. Greenland's self-governance as of 2012 meant that the island has complete authority over oil and gas and other minerals.[33] Among the latter resources are rare earths, one of the largest deposits in the world and of immense potential economic value, and critical minerals used in production of electric vehicles. Another natural resource whose possible harvesting and export raises concern from environmentalists and snickers from the general public is icebergs, which is a source of fresh water. In addition, sand that is used to feed cement production is a resource needed for industrial and commercial development.

Greenland's eventual full independence from Denmark is not unrelated to climate change. Should discoveries of oil and gas in Greenland negate the remarkable fact that not a single barrel of oil has ever been extracted—let alone exported—from Greenland, energy resources could be a basis for freeing the giant island from Denmark's current control through that nation's generous block grant program.

The diversity and variety of the Arctic was showcased in a 2018 *New York Times* travel section's focus on Nuuk: "a choice destination to take in upscale Greenlandic cuisine, stylish fashion and contemporary art and design." The *New York Times* is accurate as far as it goes and parts of the city look like a *National Geographic* photo contest winner. To sample the *Times* preferred restaurants' offerings of tapas of lamb and tarragon mayonnaise, reindeer carbonade, musk ox fillet and haunch wrapped in seaweed, non-Nuuk residents need to have some time. Trips from New York City or other major world cities to Nuuk take about 40 hours and include a stop in Iceland or Denmark.

In Nuuk, a short walk from the fancy restaurants takes you to stores selling "some of the warmest [and priciest] wool items in the world," which is in contrast with the wares laid out on the streets by people in front of fish stalls and supermarkets, such as old CDs, gloves and some handmade items. Other streets, all of which end in the city outskirts (no roads connect Nuuk to other parts of Greenland), look like an abandoned late Soviet urban neighborhood. The Danes experimented with housing for the Inuit in 1966 and 1967. In an attempt at modernization, they superimposed upon the fishing culture gigantic buildings not suited to the ways Inuit people work and fish. One building alone, Bloc P, housed 1 percent of the total population of the country. But these spaces were not compatible with the storage needs of people who fish nor were they adequate for cleaning their catches. Hence some of the buildings now serve as tourist attractions of failed planning, while others were demolished.

Life expectancy for Greenland women is 74 years; for men, 68. These numbers are about a decade shorter than for Denmark. Although suicide rates are high, the actual number is small: for example, in 2013, 25 people, mostly males under 30, killed themselves. Over time, the population at the highest risk of suicide changed from older men to men aged 15–24.

Though gigantic in mass, tiny in population, there is a lot of information available about Greenland: there are a few beehives in Greenland; there are three dozen Americans; there are a few motorcycles. In 2013, the Greenlandic government calculated that 219 people started college (which was a pretty simple statistic to chase down, since college is paid for by the government), and of those, 72 graduated. Twenty-seven got degrees in the humanities, four in natural sciences while one studied architecture. Greenland is a high-income country and has been since 1989 according to the World Bank. Average earnings per resident are about $33,000. The country's literacy rate is high. However, education is spotty as few towns have high schools, and about 60 percent of people aged 18–25 years have not completed high school or vocational training. Greenland's educational level is the lowest in the Nordic region.[34]

Since World War II, Greenland has changed from being a remote island of hunting communities to a place with commercial fishing and an embryonic but recently very active mining industry. For Greenlanders living in larger population centers like Nuuk and a handful of other towns, the standard of living is similar to Europe's. But about a quarter of Greenlanders live in small settlements without adequate emergency healthcare and schools.

To the future of the Arctic environment and to the world environment, the importance of Greenland is as big as its mass. Of great interest to the future of the Arctic environment is what happens as temperatures continue to rise, the seas and glaciers melt, and the environment changes in the ways described later. Tourism will be much easier. In the midterm, this will not mean a great number of visitors because of the high costs and limitations on movement on the gigantic land mass. Until the early 1950s, there were virtually no tourists in Greenland and even in recent years the number is fewer than 100,000 annually. With climate change, mining will be more accessible; exporting will be more affordable; plants and animals will arrive or migrate.

Greenlanders vary in their views of climate change: for example, a taxi driver greeting a visitor may say he doesn't think about it at all. And climate change does not have a special place in the school curriculum. Leaders of hunting and fishing organizations say it is difficult to get their members to discuss it.[35] High-level government leaders "know it is ongoing. We see it everywhere, but we differ on whether it is good or bad."[36] A 2018–19 study found that over 90 percent of Greenlanders believe climate change is happening, but a much smaller percentage attribute it to human activity (52 percent).[37] Among the victims or those who will be harmed by climate change, sled dogs were mentioned most often.[38] Those deeply concerned include the artists who shipped several tons of icebergs calved from a Greenland fjord to London for an art installation to show the effects of melting, prior to an international meeting on climate change.[39] Some see global warming as an opportunity, such as creation of conducive conditions for the arrival of new fish species or development of new industries. Ideas include moving giant icebergs to places needing freshwater and exporting sand to rapidly growing parts of the world where industrial grade sand is unavailable. These views provided the background for Greenland pulling out of the Paris Agreement, the most recent international effort to address climate change (described in a later chapter). On other environmental issues, the opinions of the Inuit, who have a central place in the Greenland government, vary like that of many peoples. Most feel that traditional ways have been sustainable over the centuries and rules imposed from the outside, including those on whaling and polar bears, are not needed and do not fully reflect the views of indigenous people.

Ironically called "Green land," much of the country is actually ice: ice that is massive, remarkable and filled with such huge amounts of water that it can have colossal effects worldwide depending on whether it stays in place or melts. As Elizabeth Kolbert so eloquently described:

> The ice sheet is so big—at its center, it's two miles high—that it creates its own weather. Its mass is so great that it deforms the earth, pushing the

> bedrock several thousand feet into the mantle. Its gravitational tug affects the distribution of the oceans.
>
> In recent years [...] the ice sheet has awoken from its postglacial slumber [...] This year's melt season began so freakishly early, in April, that when the data started to come in, many scientists couldn't believe it [...] Just in the past four years, more than a trillion tons of ice have been lost. This is four hundred million Olympic swimming pools' worth of water.[40]

Iceland

> A Country with the soul of a very small town.[41]

East of Greenland is Iceland, perhaps the country most associated with things Arctic. However, only a small part of Iceland, Grimsey Island, is within the Arctic Circle. Most of the country is a few degrees south of it. But other indicators make this an iconic Arctic nation. One-third of the country is desert, in contrast to when the Vikings arrived at a place of trees and grass.[42] Iceland belongs to many Arctic organizations. Its temperatures vary, but the average in the winter in the southerly lowland is about freezing. The mean temperature in Reykjavík is -0.5°C (31°F) in January. Further north, the temperatures are considerably colder. The climate is unstable, and torrential winds and rain can appear wildly throughout the year.

Iceland has very few people, but on its streets, in buses, on glaciers, and under its majestic waterfalls, one can find large numbers of tourists. Based on 2018 numbers, there are about eight visitors for every Icelander. Three hundred and thirty-eight thousand people live in Iceland, on a land mass bigger than Hungary (with about 10 million people); its population is growing by about 1.7 percent per year. Most Icelanders live in the picturesque gem of Reykjavik (with 60 percent of the total population). The rest, 120,000, live in small villages or farms or in few of the other cities, of which many are on the coast, and; here one can find several rural communities. Iceland is a place of remarkable and unique beauty. Black lava dots hills of yellow rock, and giant waterfalls provide unforgettable vistas. The country, despite a major economic downturn in 2008, is wealthy and healthy. Yet as late as the 1970s, the United Nations Development Programme (UNDP) still classified the island as a developing country, and in the period 2008–11, it suffered a massive economic collapse. The average male Icelander lives to be 80, and for women the life expectancy is four years more. Infant mortality hovers at about the lowest in Europe (1 to 2.5 percent).

Iceland's coastline is 4,970 kilometers or about 3,100 miles long. Offshore, waters in which it has considerable regulatory and management authority, are some of the richest fishing grounds in the world. Glaciers, some melting very quickly, cover one-tenth of the island and are the main source of hydropower. Recent history on sources of Iceland's energy is relevant to the sustainability of the Arctic—and potentially of other parts of the world. Its unique movement from almost total dependence on fossil fuels just decades ago to its almost exclusive use in some sectors of renewable energy sources is remarkable. Those resources include geothermal, hydropower and wind. Geothermal energy has witnessed an extraordinary and rapid development. Now the nation, having learned that it could not rely on fossil fuel imports because of their unpredictable and often high costs, powers its homes and industries through this energy source, generated through tectonic movements deep in the earth and very active volcanic grounds. The geothermal resource is now made accessible through deep drilling technology. However, almost incredibly, the move to using geothermal energy began with an individual developing a primitive system for his own farm; later a far-flung network of municipalities adopted the geothermal option. Now about 90 percent of homes in Iceland are heated directly by geothermal sources. Sustainability was further promoted by a government action that created a geothermal drilling mitigation fund, which offers grants for research and drilling tests as well as for trial projects, which do not always succeed. Municipalities face less risk in transitioning to this renewable energy source because of the subsidy.

Hydropower is produced from the massive amount of melting glaciers in Iceland as water makes its way down to the sea. It is now a source for international industry energy users, including aluminum production. Hydropower also rose from modest roots: individual Icelanders and cooperatives began building small plants to provide for their farms, over 500 were set up just in 1950. Large projects came later—some strongly opposed by many environmentalists. Iceland also has tremendous potential for tapping into wind energy resources, but efforts are still in the embryonic stage. The nation is now a leader in education and training in advocating the shift to using renewable energy resources. It shares its knowledge and experience worldwide, including through special courses made available to foreign students in its universities. These are taught along with United Nations' geothermal training programs and at higher learning institutions, such as the Iceland School of Energy at Reykjavík University.[43]

Also of considerable interest to the future of the Arctic environment is what happens as tourism increases. Iceland's tourism revenue helps fuel a robust economy, but its numbers and limited management make for environmental challenges: some are aesthetic; others can be more significant. It is not a rare day at the famous Blue Lagoon when crowds seem like those at Disneyland, and plastic cups are left sitting in the cave-like sections as visitors change from their robes and dine in restaurants that could as well be in Manhattan. Tourists arrive by plane, among the most carbon intensive ways of traveling, and this tiny country has almost 100 airports. Visitors, confronted with crowds, often the antithesis of what they were seeking, look for off road experiences.[44] Driving there damages moss-covered places and volcanic features; this accelerates erosion and expansion of deserts.[45] Large numbers of tourists also place a high demand on energy sources, which then need to be expanded in vulnerable landscapes. Also, graffiti defaces ancient sites, and the absence of tourism infrastructure leads to outdoor defecation. Places that were silent are no longer so.

Some aspects of tourism are rapidly changing. What is still billed as a gentle walk on a spectacular blue-white glacier ("Enjoy an easy Glacier Walk on Sólheimajökull glacier and visit two stunning waterfalls on this day tour from Reykjavík") may now be a white knuckle challenge. The pace of melting has been remarkable and has led to scenes of tourists—expecting to be leisurely looking at spectacular white scenes—staring into deep carved out crevices wondering how they would get up, or actually down, now. Hikers need to use their axes and walking poles having picked them up only as if that were part of the scene. A tour guide, surprised herself, found that when she was at the site last, just months earlier, the glacier was three meters deeper than now. Water swirls around, new steps need to be carved into melting ice, new caves open, and the beauty of the place is now tainted by moving mud and more and more volcanic ash.

The future of the Arctic environment is important to Iceland in several critical ways, in addition to tourism—which brings the good and the bad. What will be the effects of changing climate on its important and rich fisheries? How will differing views about the seriousness of environmental change affect the country's international relations? Powerful countries have their sights on the Arctic, and how Iceland responds is critical. Are joint projects with non-Arctic countries compatible with sustainability, however defined? Will differences over regulations of whaling or exploitation of fossil fuels damage the country's capacity to sustain the lifestyles of the wealthy and of indigenous peoples?

Norway

About half of Norway (58° N to 81° N latitude), a long narrow country, lies north of the Arctic circle. The country's Arctic population is just under

400,000 making Norway's one of the most populated Arctic regions. . But this represents only a small percentage of the total population of the country of over 5.3 million.[46]

Although cold, the country, even in its farthest reaches, has moderate temperature. The average winter temperature in Tromsø (69.65° N latitude) is about 30°F (around -1°C).

Recent years have witnessed a considerable growth in Arctic tourism. In 2017, the country received 6.3 million visitors.[47] Norway is both rich and a strong welfare state which regularly ranks among the top nations in per capita wealth, ahead of Middle Eastern powers, the United States and other Scandinavian nations. Part of the abundance comes from a remarkable national fund which invests revenue from the oil and gas industry in companies, bonds and real estate. In 2019, the fund earned the equivalent of $34,000 for each person living in Norway.[48] Some public perceptions hold that all Norwegians are rich because of the massive size of its global funds. Individuals are well taken care of under the strong Norwegian welfare system and will be for the foreseeable future but not through regular direct payments from the funds. Fund managers evaluate environmental and social implications of entities it considers investing in. The Ministry of Finance Council on Ethics reviews companies even to the point of considering divestments in activities that are considered nonsustainable (some of which conveniently also are not wise business choices.)

Norway's Arctic has several small municipalities. Bigger cities are Bodø and Tromsø—the latter the site of the Secretariat of the Arctic Council, a forum-type international organization of Arctic nations and peoples (which is discussed later in this volume). Like other Norwegian cities of the North, Tromsø is cosmopolitan, the "Paris of the Arctic," with warm, candle-lit restaurants, impressive office buildings and museums, a historical cathedral, welcoming coffee shops, a lively night scene, and a world-famous university with strong Arctic departments. Here a visitor arriving on a cold winter night will be welcomed by a waiting bus which will deliver him or her almost to the doorstep of any of the many hotels in the city.

The economy is heavily associated with fish and fisheries. It is also a country with a strong tradition of international aid and giving. Its environmental record is strong too, but in classical environmental thinking it is somewhat schizophrenic with acceptance of whaling and considerable ongoing exploitation of fossil fuels. More than 50,000 people work in industries that extract these energy sources or are in related businesses. This is not a large percentage of the workforce, but Norwegian productivity in the sector is great. Petroleum and associated activities make for almost 20 percent of the GDP of the country.[49] What's more, over half of the fuel reserves that are extractable remain untapped on the Norwegian continental shelf which means, as explained in Chapter 4, these are under Norway's control. The resource is roughly equal parts oil and gas. Under international legal obligations, Norway plans to aggressively reduce emissions at home, and yet it is expanding fossil fuel production for sale abroad. "Highly insufficient" is the way its implemented policies are described by climate change followers—consistent with warming between 3°C (5.4 F°) and 4°C (7.2°F).[50] Yet many of its policies and actions are aimed at promoting carbon neutrality.

Norway now has a comprehensive climate action plan looking to 2030; by that time, the country will reach and surpass its climate targets while promoting growth in the environmental sectors and achieve carbon neutrality.[51] Emissions will be decreased in various sectors such as transport, industrial production and the fossil fuel industry. Under the plan, Norway should surpass its assigned emission target from the EU and achieve a 45 percent reduction. Policies include taxation of greenhouse gas emissions, regulatory measures and support for new green technologies. Zero emission passenger cars and small vans and local buses are also noted in the plan, as are increases in the carbon tax rate from its current level.[52] Nonetheless, Norway continues to grant oil and gas exploration licenses, including—controversially—in the Arctic. Some environmentalists are fiercely opposed, arguing that polar drilling is incompatible with global climate targets.

The Norwegian population is healthy and life expectancy is about 83.5 years.[53] Norwegians are highly educated, but a statistic relevant to the Arctic is that there is a significant percentage of people who do not complete upper secondary school (over 30 percent). Failure to do so has been linked to mental health problems and (in northernmost counties) with high populations of Sámi people, the nation's major indigenous group.

Sweden

By all indicators, Sweden is an Arctic nation. Arctic Sweden, Swedish Lapland or "the Northern Lands" encompasses about one-third of the country's area. Fifteen percent of Sweden's total land area is north of the Arctic Circle. The average northern Sweden temperature in winter is around 10°C (14°F). There are about 657,000 Arctic Swedes, representing 6.5 percent of Sweden's population. The Sámi are the main indigenous peoples of Sweden with an estimated population of 20,000 to 40,000.

The average life expectancy in Sweden is 82 years; for women it is 84 years, and 81 for men. These numbers for the Sámi are similar to those of the majority population. The Sámi lifestyle with its diet, physical activity and cultural closeness is thought to reduce the risks of certain diseases. While not as wealthy as its neighbor Norway, Sweden ranks relatively high in per capita earnings.

The story of Kiruna opens a window into Arctic Sweden.[54] The city of 17,000 people situated 100 miles north of the Arctic Circle is being physically moved a few kilometers east—this remarkable relocation is to be completed by 2023. A large majority of Kiruna's citizens (80 percent) support the move. It is required because the city is sinking and crumbling. The physical shifts is a result of mining in the large, very profitable site (half a billion dollars in revenue annually) that employs 10 percent of the city's population. Over the years, the successful iron ore extraction industry, in one of the purest and largest deposits anywhere, left gaps in the ground, and consequently, the city is becoming uninhabitable in parts. The historic all-wood cathedral, Kiruna Church, is being moved; so too are the old train station and the railroad. Houses are being built in the new Kiruna, and shopping districts are being planned. While mining has its deleterious impacts on the environment, Kiruna's mine has been the economic engine of the region. But as for other villages, cities and communities facing dramatic changes—many of which are environmental—in the Arctic, transplanting a place's culture is not easy.

Of great interest to the sustainability of the Arctic is Sweden's very strong—and yet not totally consistent—record of environmental leadership. International environmental law virtually began by an initiative proposed by the Swedes. In 1972, the Stockholm United Nations Conference on the Human Environment saw 113 countries come together to address the role of the United Nations in addressing acid rain, a leading environmental news item of the day, and other regional and global environmental threats. Now Sweden leads in combatting climate change. In 2017, it adopted a new climate policy framework and is poised to be the first country to reach the United Nations Sustainable Development Goals, described in Chapter 4. It is regularly ranked among the world's most sustainable countries. Today Sweden produces less than 0.2 percent of total global greenhouse gas emissions, and it aims to reach zero net emissions by 2050. Yet Sweden has been criticized for its failure to effectively regulate logging of its significant boreal forest and allowing clear cutting in its northern region. According to the World Wildlife Foundation (WWF), there are many forest-dwelling species (around 2,000 in number) under threat in Sweden. Also, ongoing urbanization is linked to waste run off. Farming also is a source of some weaknesses in the overall environmental record. Sweden also suffers from pollution from other countries which affects the country's air.

Finland

Most of Finland's population of 5.5 million people are not in the Arctic. Only about 180,000 people live in Lapland which is, for many, synonymous with the Finnish Arctic, and encompasses about one-third of the country. The Arctic Circle crosses Lapland at about the same latitude as Rovaniemi, Finland's thirteenth most populated city, and emblematic of Arctic Finland. It is home to a major Arctic science center Arktikum and universities (the University of Lapland and Lapland University of Applied Sciences specializing in various Arctic studies). Nearby, Santa's village attracts almost a half million visitors each year: "The official hometown of Santa Claus."

Finland is Arctic as defined in other ways too. The Finnish Arctic winter is cold and snowy. The average temperatures range in the coldest time of winter months from -22°C (-7.6°F) to -3°C (26.6°F). It is sometimes much colder, once dropping to -51°C (-59.8°F). Traditional activities associated with the Arctic include reindeer herding and raising. And Finland is actively involved in many Arctic organizations, both international and regional. Finns speak of "Snow-How" while describing their strong contributions to technological innovations that help people to lead active lives in the Far North. The country prides itself on Arctic design, construction and innovation. Finland, along perhaps with Russia, has built more icebreakers than any other country, and Finland does so both for itself and for other countries. Finland is the home of about 10,000 Sámi people, and the Finish government controls a very large part of the Sámi homeland.[55]

Strolling or fighting the winds and snow or rain on Rovaniemi's downtown plaza one can dine on Thai, Indian, Chinese or American food in a pricey restaurant. Outside of the city, dinner may be in an ice restaurant or in a teepee, where one can savor roasted elk and parsnip puree. Or a Lappish picnic might accompany the chasing of the aurora borealis. Then there are the snowmobile barbeques. Back in the city are poker and blackjack games as well as Finnish slot machines in Feel Vegas. The Arctic Snow Hotel is nearby as is a zoo with Arctic animals and a snow castle.

Of great interest to the future of the Arctic environment, Finland has been a strong leader in sustainable development in the region. The country is ranked among the world's most stringent when evaluated by environmental protection standards. Yet Finland's "ecological footprint" is higher than some other Arctic nations. And while overall greenhouse gas emissions are low when evaluated by the size of the small population, they are quite high in global terms. (Lapland's carbon dioxide emissions are under 2.8 million tons per year compared to

Finland's almost 57 million tons annually.) Finland's then new government said in 2019 that the country will aim to cut its carbon emissions completely by 2035. And later it decided to ban the use of coal in energy production by 2029.

The region sees climate change as a threat to traditional lifestyles while also a source of economic development opportunity. Its strategic position geographically and its history with Russia are important to the future Arctic. Finland plays an important role in periods of tension between Russia and the United States and other Arctic and near Arctic nations.

Russia

Bordering Finland on the east is the Russian Federation. Though thousands of miles away, one is still in Arctic Russia, Siberia. There in the large city of Yakutsk, coming out of an underground museum filled with permanent ice sculptures of modern celebrities and ancient icons, one crosses streets with ski slope sized moguls, the surface having shifted because of thawing. Although difficult to identify for the non-Russian speaker, along the streets, behind weather protection walls, are many jewelry shops where diamonds are a specialty. Giant statues of Lenin sit in main squares overlooking the frozen center. High-rises and some covered in rust—tower above the traditional wooden long houses, of which many are sinking into the land. The Russian Arctic is not only Siberia—gigantic, it includes islands and Arctic seas: the Kara, the Laptev, the Chukchi and the East Siberian. Also, the Bering Sea and the Sea of Okhotsk are in the ocean zones of Russia, where, under international law, the Russian Federation has certain rights. Russia's Arctic territory stretches along 24,140 kilometers (about 15,000 miles) of coastline accounting for 53 percent of Arctic Ocean coastline.

Russia's Arctic and sub-Arctic territories are the world's coldest, with the exception of Antarctica. The Yakutsk region regularly sees temperatures below -50°C (-58°F) and saw a record low -71.2°C (-96.16°F) in 1924. Daily average low temperatures during winter range from -20°C (-4°F) to -40°C (-40°F). Yet in 2018, the Russian northern coastal regions experienced temperatures above 30°C (86°F) and reached 100°F (38°C) in one city in June 2020.

Russia is a major presence in the Arctic in almost all ways. About one-fifth of the Russian land mass is north of the Arctic Circle: 5.5 million square kilometers or about 2 million square miles. Roughly 2.8 million people live in Arctic Russia—almost three-quarters of the Arctic population. The indigenous peoples of the area are said to have developed genetic differences that allow them and their cultures to cope with the extreme environment.[56] In the mid-2000s in

Russia's Arctic region, a natural increase of the population began; however, the overall population is declining (as it is elsewhere in Russia, this is a source of considerable concern, including for the administration under President Putin, with implications for development pushes in the Arctic). International migration continues with foreign laborers leading the movement. Russia is a member of several of the international Arctic organizations and undertakes considerable Arctic research both with and independent of other Arctic nations.

Unlike those of the other Arctic Eight, Russian cities in the North have large populations: Yakutsk, 311,760; Murmansk, 295,374; Petropavlovsk-Kamchatsky, 181,216; and Norilsk, 179,554.[57] The average annual income of their people differs considerably. While that of the Russian Federation as a whole is about $12,000, income differences within the Russian Arctic are wider. Defense industry jobs generally pay well for the region. In the Republic of Sakha (Yakutia), 8,500 kilometers, or about 5,300 miles, from Moscow (now reachable by train including many hundreds of kilometers over permafrost), the average yearly income is 50,000 rubles or $7,500.

Life expectancy in the Russian Federation as a whole is about 72 years. As of 2018, there is a great spread, of about 10 years between the shorter lived men and the women—larger than for other Arctic nations. Within Arctic Russia, there is some variability: life expectancy is shortest in Chukotka (62.8 years). In general it is shorter in the Russian Arctic than in the other Arctic regions where health challenges are greatest such as the incidence of tuberculosis.

By non-Arctic and even by non-Russian Arctic standards, conditions in the Russian Arctic are challenging. But there is pride among many inhabitants about the ability to live and thrive in the Far North. As said about the "people from the North":

> The Severyane [Northerners] have unique qualities: fulfilled in their work, they are not afraid of physical challenges, and are hospitable and sharing because Arctic conditions lead to solidarity. They carry the virtues of late socialism, such as personal fulfillment, and curb consumerism. They are often embodied by geologists or specialized engineers—heroes of Soviet industrialization—and celebrate gender equality and women's success in traditionally male-dominated professions.[58]

The Arctic Russian economy is dependent on natural resources: nickel, copper, coal, gold, uranium, tungsten and diamonds, and there are vast reserves of fossil fuel which Russian governments work to exploit. Ninety percent of Russia's oil and gas reserves are in the Arctic, further leading the country to promote the Northern Sea Route for oil transport to Asia. Billions of dollars are being invested for infrastructure development in the Russian Arctic.[59] Some of these initiatives have considerable military value, which raises concerns for some observers outside of Russia about the implications for long-term cooperation in the region.

The future of the Russian Arctic environment is of great significance to the Arctic. Considerable thawing of the permafrost, dramatic in Arctic Russia, is changing the ways Russians in the North must live. At the same time, it is also exacerbating problems of climate change worldwide through the release of greenhouse gases. How oil exploitation and production is managed will also be crucial. It came as a huge surprise to the Russian authorities, or at least so reported, and a cautionary statement to the world when one of the biggest oil spills in history occurred near Norilsk, Russia, in 2020. In late May, a storage tank failed and about 20,000 metric tons of diesel fuel spilled into the Ambarnaya River and its environs making its way to the Arctic Ocean. The collapse of the facility was caused at least in part by the thawing of the permafrost at its foundation. Early speculation set the time for restoration of the aquatic environment at a decade.[60]

Russia has not solved the problem of nuclear pollution of the Arctic originating from its Cold War activities there. Statements, including from the Russian Academy of Science and Oceanology, conclude that there has been no contamination from leaks from the submarines and thousands of containers (perhaps 17,000), reactors and heavy machinery dumped for decades beginning in 1955 by the Russian Navy. That these self-reports are accurate has not been established. The country has had a dominant position in manufacturing and using great nuclear powered ships. By 2003, it had built almost 250 submarines and several other vessels powered by around 450 reactors. Nuclear-powered vessels including icebreakers can be used to foster activities that protect the ocean. They can also facilitate explorations for oil and other resources. These ships need to be managed extremely carefully in the conditions of the frozen sea to avoid environmental damage and loss of human life. The environmental challenges remain major memories after the nuclear-powered *Kursk* accident in the Barents Sea in 2000. During a Russian naval exercise, all the crew of the submarine (118 people) died after two explosions on board, the source of which remains not certain. The submarine was built in 1994.[61]

The United States

The American Arctic is Alaska. But not all Alaska is Arctic: most commonly accepted as Arctic are the North Slope Borough, the Northwest Arctic Borough, and the Nome Census area, Prudhoe Bay, Barrow, Kotzebue, Nome, and Galena. American Arctic indicators other than latitude include its indigenous peoples: as of 2014, Alaska's 20 indigenous languages have official status; these belong mainly to two language groups or families depending on the expert conclusion.[62] Language families include Inuit-Unangan or Eskimo-Aleut and Na-Dene (or Athabasan-Eyak-Tingit). Native peoples represent about 14 to 15 percent of the 735,000 people in the gigantic state. The US Census in 2010 estimated the Alaskan native population resident in Alaska to be roughly 138,300 (figures which appear to have roughly held in preliminary analysis of the 2020 census).[63] These Alaskan natives belong to the Inuit, Tlingit, Haida, Alaska Athabaskan, Aleut and other tribal groupings.[64]

Temperatures too have historically been Arctic or extreme in the North: long cold winters (the average annual low for Barrow is -14°C [6.4°F]). One year, the temperature dropped to a record -80°F (-62°C) in Prospect Creek. The state is part of the US organizations that represent the country in Arctic international organizations. Alaskan indigenous peoples belong to international Arctic organizations that include other indigenous people. Also an Arctic characteristic is the fact that the landscapes are tundra and permafrost.[65]

Alaska, where one can drive for hours on comfortable gravel and dirt roads without encountering not more than a dozen human beings, is gigantic. These roads do not lead to many communities, and these some can be reached only by snowmobiles or by air during certain times of the year. The land is diverse: snow-covered mountains look down on clear tumbling rivers and awe-inspiring herds of majestic animals—caribou, grizzlies, polar bears, wolverines and seals. Contrastingly, one can also find here frontier bars that welcome patrons with bright neon lights as well as uninteresting commercial streets that stretch out of town—which could be anywhere in the drabbest parts of the Lower 48. Both parts of Alaska are home for Alaska residents.

Alaskan Arctic social conditions are varied. The life expectancy of Alaskan natives was 47 years in 1950; it increased to over 69 years in 2000 compared to the average for all US residents of 77 years.[66] Poverty in the US Arctic is considerable, but it is mitigated by a program—funded by wealth generated by oil rents—which provides what is called universal basic income to all residents, although recently it has lost some of its capacity to reduce poverty.[67] Alaska natives remain several times more likely to be poor and out of work than other Alaskans. They also have high rates of accidental deaths, suicides, alcoholism, homicides, fetal alcohol syndrome and domestic violence, and while they make up only a small percentage of Alaska's residents, over one-third of its prison population are Alaskan natives, with an imprisonment rate almost double the nationwide average.

The beauty of Arctic attracts 2 million visitors, who travel here mostly by plane and by ship (about 1.5 million in cruises) each year. Many come to experience the glaciers which tourists travel to by kayaks, ferryboats or gondolas.[68] Tourists bring business. In 2016, the 70,000-ton *Crystal Serenity*, with a capacity to carry 1,600 passengers, first visited villages a fraction of its size; three dozen other ships were also docked nearby. Where and how ships dock affects the livelihoods of villagers. Passengers come with currency, create expectations of business, bring, depending on how regulated, noise and waste as well as unknown species on their crafts.

Also of great interest to the future of the Arctic environment are planned activities of oil exploration and possible exploitation. Of most importance is the almost 20 million acre (78 million square kilometers) Arctic National Wildlife Refuge, commonly known as ANWR, which is a politically charged place as the government is considering drilling for oil in one of its subsections, which makes up only a very small percentage of its territory. Will development go forward in a way that protects its wildlife, the remarkable scenery and pristine air quality? Will it go forward at all? Will its exploitation help or hinder sustaining how Alaska people live?[69]

Similar questions are raised for some mining projects. One, not within the Arctic itself, involves a potentially immensely valuable source of copper, gold and other metals, the Pebble Mine. Located southwest of Anchorage, this was favored by the Trump administration; over its two-decade history, however, this project has drawn opposition from both Republican and Democratic leaders. In 2020, a permit for its operation was denied but attempts to develop may continue.[70] The question of the meanings of sustainability was suggested by the title of a newspaper article describing the conflict over going forward: "A Clash of Buried Treasure and Living Treasure in Alaska."[71] Estimates are that the mine's resources may be worth more than $300 billion. Northern Dynasty Minerals, the Canadian developer, would employ about 1,000 people to work on the open-pit mine, roads and pipelines in the Iliamma area.

Some native corporations, entities established after land claims resolutions (described later in the volume), had planned to try and stop the project, including by refusing entry to their land. They are concerned about loss of salmon fisheries (one of the largest in the world, and the sockeye salmon run is the largest in the world); the possible damages that could come from failure of high dams following volcanic activity or earthquakes; and other effects on the economic, cultural and ecological value of Bristol Bay.[72] Dams need to be built as part of the project. But other village corporations had agreed to permit access to almost 70,000 acres. According to one mine supporter, this group "doesn't see Iliamma surviving without a project like Prebble."[73]

The Alaskan future confronts other questions: As climate change continues to affect the Arctic in dramatic ways, what will happen to Alaskan villages whose shorelines are falling into the sea and whose residents are facing evacuation? Will caribou and polar bear find enough to eat? Will they be able to move and migrate with changes in terrain and temperature? Will rules be adapted to preserve the traditions of indigenous peoples, whalers and sealers, while also protecting vulnerable animals?

The indigenous peoples of Alaska will be involved in determining the fate of the Arctic. There is no consensus, and they do not act in a concerted manner. Some are content with roles in their corporations, while others, in their own view, remain outsiders. One of the respondents in our Arctic Survey summarized this view:

> I am a descendant of this land. We have documented management of this land over 14,000 years. We are 8 percent of the prison age population, however we are 42 percent of Alaska's prison population. As a group we are the largest landowners in America, yet we do not have the right to manage wildlife on our own lands. Let us heal our lands and we will heal.

For Alaska, the key to understanding the future of the Arctic environment is its indigenous peoples. To appreciate the historical relationship between dominant rule makers and native peoples as well as the present influence of the indigenous requires a primer on some history, namely that of indigenous peoples with Russia, the United States and the state of Alaska.

The first Europeans to arrive in Alaska were Russian explorers. They encountered native peoples—some nomadic, others more settled. The territory was occupied by the Russian Empire for well over a century. In 1867, under the presidency of Andrew Johnson, the United States bought Alaska from Russia leading to the coining of the phrase "Seward's Folly" or "Seward's Icebox" because Secretary of State William Seward negotiated the treaty for the transfer. The federal government then began to impose restrictions on indigenous Alaskans' activities and rights including to education, voting and religious practice. Treatment was similar to that of native Americans in other parts of the United States. And the effects were similar: dependency on government income transfers, poverty, educational failure, health problems, teenage suicide and loss of cultural practices.

In 1959, Alaska became a state. The state government contends that, historically, indigenous Alaskans have always been seen as individuals and not peoples. There are no treaties, and only a few reservation lands exist. (Instead of by formal treaties, agreements with tribes after 1871 were made by US executive branch representatives and presented to Congress for adoption.[74]) Upon statehood, a federation of indigenous peoples that was formed filed land claims to all of Alaska. These claims became all the more important after the discovery of oil in Alaska in 1968. Three years later, the US Congress passed the Alaskan Native Claims Settlement Act (ANCSA) extinguishing indigenous titles. In their stead, corporations were created throughout Alaska and almost a billion dollars and 180,000 square kilometers of land were distributed among indigenous Alaskans. But many Alaska natives widely criticized ANCSA for imposing a corporate structure over their traditional forms of governance. And the act did not recognize subsistence hunting and fishing rights. In 1988, amendments were made to the act; in its corporate effects, stock sale restrictions and tax exemptions were extended indefinitely, and corporations were authorized to issue new stock to younger people and non-indigenous people. Still not all Alaskan natives approved these changes. While some members of the Alaska Federation of Natives (AFN) welcomed them in part because the amendments could encourage economic development, others saw these as threats to traditional lifestyles and rights. Then, in 1980, rights, including traditional uses of resources, were recognized in the Alaska National Interest Lands Conservation Act, which also set aside land for wildlife refuges and national parks. The act is administered mainly by the state, so the potential for conflicts about priorities continued. However, in 1993, the federal Bureau of Indian Affairs confirmed 225 Alaskan villages as recognized tribes. Several regional corporations have now transferred their lands to tribal governments to protect them against state appropriation.

Environmental quality and sustainability are points of contention among indigenous peoples, some Alaskans and, more generally, other Americans. Native people experience the effects in direct and very disruptive ways. Their hunting patterns need to be changed; ice-based activities are disrupted if not precluded; some villages are disappearing and in need of relocation because of massive erosion of shoreline; drilling challenges subsistence way of life. Yet, oil companies generate state revenue for Alaska, and this creates wealth for Alaskans. Oil exploration is controversial both inside and outside native communities. Among the most contentious cases is drilling in ANWR where there is a clash between the Gwich'in and Inupiat viewpoints.[75]

There are several other examples of different understandings of sustainability that arise from environmentalists' challenges to traditional practices.

Regulations in the fur industry and to support limitations on sales of walrus ivory fossils and artwork (this is one of the strategic attempts to protect elephants slaughtered for their ivory) are opposed by some indigenous peoples. Further, there are ongoing differences on whaling. While major differences in the interpretations of the rights of indigenous peoples to take whales have been, for the most part, resolved at the government and indigenous tribe levels, questions remain. International and US law prohibit the killing of certain whale species, but allow hunting of some species by indigenous peoples. And bowhead whales have been hunted by indigenous people in Alaska for centuries. Traditional subsistence hunts are legal under federal law (the Marine Mammal Protection Act) with hunting allowed for registered members of the Alaska Eskimo Whaling Commission (AEWC). The Inuit Circumpolar Conference, an Arctic Inuit-wide organization that Alaska indigenous peoples are part of—holds that native hunting should not be included in the US quota of whale killings. Hence, although lessened at times, tensions do persist over differences in interpretations. And there are ongoing challenges to the degree of commitment of US enforcement, including those made by environmental and animal protection organizations.

Canada

Canada meets all of the indicators of an Arctic nation. Much of Canada is Arctic by latitude. Maps of the Arctic published by the Canadian government show a boundary encompassing over 40 percent of Canada's landmass and 25 percent of the global Arctic. The Canadian Arctic includes the low-lying tundra of the Arctic coastal plains. There is permafrost and polar deserts at high latitudes. To the south of the tree line are boreal forests. There is one road in North America that leads to the Arctic Ocean, and this is in Canada. A product of a joint venture between two indigenous-owned construction and transportation companies, the road opened in 2017.[76] Canadian and indigenous peoples' governments belong to many Arctic organizations. Canada's North has cold winters, with averages ranging from -20°C (-4°F) to -35°C (-31°F.)[77] The Canadian Arctic has a population of about 100,000—density very different from that of the southernmost urban areas of Canada.

Social conditions in the Canadian Arctic are varied.[78] Suicide rates are high in the Canadian Arctic, with the rates among indigenous communities being higher than those of the general Canadian population. Inuit rates rank among the world's highest. In one period (1999–2003) suicides in Inuit regions averaged at 135 per 100,000; over 10 times that of Canada in general. The Inuit rate has increased considerably in recent years. Major contributors were dramatic increases in suicide by younger people and the loss of cultural continuity.[79] Young women are more often victims to suicide in Canada.

While the health of indigenous peoples has improved in recent years, major problems remain, including a high infant mortality rate. Tuberculosis is still a serious problem: the Inuit have a rate almost 300 times that of non-indigenous people. Housing conditions also are below acceptable standards in some areas, with people living in overcrowded conditions in dwellings that need major repairs.[80] Over three-fourths of the youth of Nunavut do not finish high school, and funding for indigenous children's school lags considerably behind funding for other schools in Canada.[81] The Northern territories—Nunavut, the Northwest Territories and Yukon—have an economic growth rate that is somewhat higher than the national average.

One sticking point in the relationship between Canada and the Arctic is the country's views and polices on the Northwest Passage—namely, waterways of the Canadian Arctic Archipelago, Canadian islands north of the Canada's mainland. Bluntly put, Canada claims these are Canadian territorial waters under international law, and there has been an established history including use by Inuit of these waters. This for Canadians is nonnegotiable: the waterways are just like the country's internal lakes and rivers. The United States, until recently a major critic of this view (with the opening of Arctic waters, other nations have become interested), considers the waters as "international straits." Under international rules, they are open to innocent movement of shipping traffic. Each side makes its case relying on well-known international law cases on ocean boundaries (commonly known as the *Corfu Channel* and the *Fisheries* cases)—predictably with different outcomes. The United States has been willing to agree to disagree on the question, as have the Canadians. The peaceful relations among the North American neighbors make this resolution acceptable now, but if less-friendly nations take the official position of the United States, more conflicts could arise.

Indigenous peoples

There are more than 600 recognized First Nations bands in Canada as well as nonstatus and urban indigenous populations, Metis and Inuit peoples. Inuit are the original people of the North American Arctic. There are about 60,000 Inuit in Canada, just over 4 percent of the Aboriginal population of around 1.7 million.[82] They are members of nine main Inuit groups who are descendants of the Thule people, who lived in the Arctic from 400 to 1,000 years ago. Innu, Dene and Cree are among the other indigenous peoples.[83]

How understanding of Arctic sustainability is linked to indigenous peoples has played out centrally and significantly in Canada. To appreciate the present relationship between historically dominant rule makers and native peoples, one needs to know about Canada's history of indigenous peoples. It is a dark and ugly one, although it did not begin that way. And it has changed. It involves settler-articulated cooperation including for instrumental reasons such as land claims and transfers as well as massive governmental and church attempts of assimilation and cultural eradication.

Under early treaties between indigenous peoples and French and British governments (1676–1763), indigenous peoples were recognized for their trade value but they were also exploited. Treaties of this era focused on land ownership, promised peace and friendship, guaranteed the indigenous the rights to trade and hunt, and pledged, in the case of the British, regular supplies from the Crown. The British increased their investment in indigenous relationships in part because the Crown knew that their French enemies had strong ties to the indigenous peoples.

After the British defeat of the French, the 1763 Royal Proclamation determined how the British would interact with indigenous peoples. This position was affirmed in 1982 in a section of the Constitution Act, principles of which are still used today. The proclamation claimed "dominion" and "sovereignty" over indigenous territories and allowed only for the Crown to make treaties with indigenous peoples.

Following the British Conquest (Great Britain's acquisition of Canada during the Seven Years' War), the British government saw indigenous peoples as valuable allies against Americans during the American Revolution and the War of 1812. These alliances also gave the British access to more territories that they used for white settlement and development. (The 1783 Treaty of Paris that concluded the American Revolution had ignored earlier treaties between the Crown and indigenous peoples who were not invited to the negotiations of the treaty.)

The North-West Company (NWC,) a fur trading company headquartered in Montreal, expanded the influence of British imperialism and Canadian commerce over more indigenous territory by further developing the trade network and strengthening ties between the Crown and indigenous peoples. This expansion led to competition with the Hudson Bay Company (HBC), another royally chartered fur trading business, which had developed extensive and elaborate relations in the region.

Several indigenous confederacies came to prominence in the late eighteenth and early nineteenth centuries, but they ultimately disintegrated in battles.

Between 1781 and 1862, about 30 treaties (also known as the Upper Canada Land Surrenders) were signed, which helped provide Loyalists with lands to settle after the American Revolution. However, to the indigenous peoples, many of these treaties were unjust appropriation of land with meager compensation, use of unclear treaty terms and policies that fostered racial segregation. The Robinson Treaties of 1850 advanced the concept of reserves, setting a precedent for treaty negotiators in the nineteenth and twentieth centuries.

When Canada became independent in 1867, it inherited obligations under treaties between First nations, as sovereign nations, and the British Crown. But Canada's intentions and interpretations of those agreements were different from that of the indigenous people. Canada proceeded to limit the self-governance of First Nations peoples, their control over indigenous lands, and education and health care services. The newly formed Canada was intent on expanding west and north to secure the nation's standing, and to that end, it signed many treaties. Later, indigenous relationships were increasingly managed by the federal Indian Act of 1876. As later amended, it aimed to assimilate First Nations and it provided for government control of Indian status, land, resources, wills and education.

These treaties were marked by the Canadian government as legally assuming responsibility for the "protection" and "well-being" of indigenous peoples, as well as compensating them for Canadian interests in traditional territories. Efforts to develop the treaty system were motivated less by concern for indigenous rights than by economic interests. Some indigenous peoples saw these treaties as assistance in transitioning to a new way of life, but many government promises were broken. In response to indigenous peoples pushing the government to "recognize errors in some early colonial treaties," investigations and findings of a commission instituted to look into the matter led to the Williams Treaties in 1923. These also became subject to different interpretations; however the principal aim was to transfer lands for cash from First Nations to the Canadian and Ontario governments while guaranteeing continuing indigenous rights to hunt and fish. (The interpretations about harvesting rights were not resolved until 2018.)[84]

Human rights play an important part in the history of struggle of indigenous peoples of Canada. Over many decades, governments acted to deny the validity of many elements of indigenous culture, requiring schooling of a particular kind (The Residential School System) and restricting use of native languages. Residential schools were found throughout Canada including in the Arctic where there were 35 schools: 16 in the Northwest Territories, 13 in Nunavut and 6 in Yukon.[85] Duncan Campbell Scott ran the residential education system in

Canada for some years. His view reflected a prevailing attitude toward assimilation of indigenous peoples. In 1920, with the government requiring every child to attend school, he said:

> I want to get rid of the Indian problem. I do not think, as a matter of fact, that the country ought to continuously protect a class of people who are able to stand alone [...] Our objective is to continue until there is not a single Indian in Canada that has not been absorbed into the body politic and there is no Indian question, and no Indian Department, that is the whole object of the law.[86]

Though not universally interpreted this way, Scott's statement is linked to the conclusion "Kill the Indian, save the man." The First Peoples were to be eradicated as distinct nations and cultures. Independent of conclusions about the complexity of motivations, the residential schools were often places of sickness and death for students often removed hundreds of kilometers from their families. A Truth and Reconciliation Commission of Canada later called these acts "cultural genocide." For over a century, the central goals of Canada's aboriginal policy were to eliminate aboriginal governments; ignore aboriginal rights; terminate the treaties; and cause aboriginal peoples to cease to exist as distinct legal, social, cultural, religious and racial entities in Canada. While the full effects of these policies in the Arctic are still being uncovered, even preliminary results show that hundreds of deaths were recorded and unmarked graves are still being discovered.

The modern era of relations between Canadian governments and indigenous peoples is associated with the 1975 James Bay Agreement, frequently considered Canada's first modern-day treaty. Following this treaty, agreements in the 1990s and early 2000s enabled indigenous peoples to create municipal and corporate structures and to participate as shareholders in activities to exploit natural resources.

The discovery of oil in the northern regions of Canada during the 1960s and 1970s stimulated aboriginal groups to bring several land claims against the Alaskan and Canadian governments. Among these, efforts by the Tungavik Federation of Nunavut, after 13 years of intense negotiation, led to the 1992 Land Claims Agreement. As part of the agreement, the Inuit insisted on the creation of a new territory. Following Canadian government's inaction, the Inuit forced the government to put the question on a plebiscite. Fifty-three percent of the voting public favored the division.

In 1993, the Inuit and representatives of the federal government reached an agreement that produced two acts of the Canadian Parliament. The first, the Nunavut Land Claims Agreement Act, settled Inuit land claims against the government by giving the Inuit outright control of more than 135,000 square miles (350,000 square kilometers) of territory.[87] It also provided cash payments from the federal government over a 14-year period. The second, the Nunavut Act, established the territory of Nunavut out of the eastern portion of the Northwest Territories. With these actions, the Inuit also gained a share of mineral, oil, and gas development revenue as well as the rights to participate in decisions regarding the land and water resources to harvest wildlife on their lands. Importantly, regarding future activities linked to varying understandings of sustainability, the Inuit now can negotiate directly with industry about the development of nonrenewable resources on Inuit-owned lands. Also trust funds were established for the Inuit people and National Parks were created in their territory.

In April 1999, Nunavut separated from the Northwest Territories to become the newest and northernmost Canadian territory.[88] The importance of self-government agreements to the future of the Arctic is considerable. Additional understandings and interpretations of sustainability and of protection of the Arctic are now a part of decisions affecting its future.

CANADA AND CLIMATE CHANGE

Of great interest to the future of the Arctic environment are Canada's plans on international cooperation on climate change. The country's history here has been a bit of a roller coaster ride. Some controversial decisions such as for exploiting the oil sands of Alberta are not consistent with Canada's at times leadership role in international climate change lawmaking. The importance of initiatives of some of the provinces, including B.C. and Quebec, as is the case for states in the United States, will also help determine the strength of climate law aimed at protecting Canada's and the total Arctic. And involvement of indigenous peoples in Canada in international climate change rules is an ongoing point of discussion, the outcome of which will influence which senses of a sustainable Arctic prevail.

THE NON-ARCTIC ARCTIC

The countries and people visited above are those of the Arctic. As we saw in Chapter 1, other nations want international influence in the region. But the future of the Arctic will result from much more than the actions of countries. Tourists, investors, entrepreneurs and businesses—both established and new—matter both politically and as major contributors to the Arctic economy. Where and how they invest, how they travel, what they do in the Arctic, how they prioritize sustaining traditions and cultures as well as environmental quality also in some part will determine the future of the Arctic.

Non-Arctic countries and their industries are investing considerably in the region, but not evenly; some countries and regions are sought over others. China has invested in a major way: billions in assets, cooperative agreements, financing agreements or other projects—heavily in energy and the minerals industry and in infrastructure. China's companies provide a significant portion of investment capital.[89] In the five-year period beginning in 2012, the Chinese have invested $1.5 trillion in Canada. China accounts for about half of the demand for the country's minerals, buys massive amounts of timber and has important mining investments. China has also invested in Norway ($379 billion) and the United States (almost $19 billion). In 2018, China Petroleum & Chemical Corporation or Sinopec, which is a state-owned Chinese oil and gas enterprise, signed a nonbinding joint development agreement with the Alaska Gasoline Development Corporation.

In 2012, China began investing in Greenland, which now receives almost 11 percent of its GDP from China. Among the investments are for a mine for rare earth elements and uranium in southern Greenland and an iron mine near the capital, Nuuk. Greenlanders generally welcome the monies, but there have been a couple controversial investment attempts. One was a Chinese effort to buy a defunct US naval base in Greenland and another (of $550 million) was to build a new, or refurbish the existing, airport outside Nuuk and two other airfields. Denmark rejected these offers after the United States urged Copenhagen to halt the Chinese initiative. And as to the rare earth business agreement, Chinese companies may still provide the technology for mining but concern raised by the United States and the EU over Chinese control over significant amounts of these valuable mineral resources (and the link of rare earth mining to radioactive exposures) have led to a slowdown of direct business activity in this sector with the Chinese.[90]

In Iceland, the Chinese government has invested $1.2 billion, about 6 percent of the country's average GDP.[91] Much of this commitment came after China and Iceland entered a bilateral energy accord in 2012 and a free trade agreement the following year.[92] In 2015, Chinese automaker Geely invested in an Icelandic methane company, and in 2016, the Chinese government funded a Northern Lights research facility. Two years later, Iceland entered a $250 million deal to provide China with geothermal expertise. Huawei, the Chinese telecom giant, is working with Icelandic mobile phone companies to test 5G technology.

In the Russian Arctic, state-backed firms have dominated development of energy. But industry analysts expect Western petroleum companies to provide the technology required (such as extended reach drilling) and management expertise, as demonstrated by the partnership of ExxonMobil and Rosneft, a very large global public oil and gas company. International political tensions have recently slowed or obstructed quick fruition of cooperation but economic pressures continue to lead to joint activities across nations.[93]

Asian capital investments have in part made up for the reduction in US and European Arctic investments in Russia in recent years. Here too Chinese interest in the region has been particularly strong. Notably, Chinese state-owned companies have obtained up to 30 percent stakes in some joint ventures. Russia has historically been reluctant to accept major investment by the Chinese. But economic sanctions (imposed following some of Russia's international actions seen as overly aggressive by the West) has persuaded Russia to consider giving majority stakes to Chinese companies in key strategic fields and to seek partnership opportunities. Since 2013, Vladimir Putin and Xi Jinping have met more than 30 times. During a visit in June 2019, the two presidents announced $20 billion in business activities to boost economic ties, including in the Arctic, with plans to increase the annual volume of trade between the two countries to $200 billion in the coming years. A major activity in Sabetta located northeast of the Yamal Peninsula, north of the Arctic Circle. And China is involved in building an LNG transshipment terminal in Kamchatka to transport LNG from the Arctic to Asia.[94] India and Vietnam have also made investment agreements with Russia.

The UK has a long history of economic activity in the Arctic. London is the headquarters of a number of major international energy companies including Shell and BP (which owns a 20 percent stake in Rosneft) and some smaller oil firms. UK businesses also have interests in tourism, telecommunications, satellite technology and airships. Multinational companies in the Arctic are influential; Shell's Arctic spending, for example, is greater than that of many countries. The UK government has also invested in Arctic science; since 2010, the UK Research Council has committed more than £30 million in funding.

RECREATIONAL TRAVEL

Beiji!, Arctic Arctic!

Title of a documentary about the Arctic being a favorite destination for Chinese travelers

Recreational travel is an important influence on sustainability of the Arctic. Tourism, depending on its forms, brings economic goods and environmental recognition (or damage). In fact non-Arctic visitors are the main source of human presence in the Arctic; the region receives about 10.2 million visitors annually. Despite many parts of the Arctic not being easily accessible and traveling conditions being extreme at times, tourism continues to grow. The Arctic has diverse forms of mass and passive tourism, fishing and hunting, adventure and extreme sports, and ecological and cultural exploration.

Almost 1 million tourists annually visit the Russian Arctic. Were it not for visa requirements, border controls and other impediments to travel planning, a discretionary activity, the numbers would be greater. One thousand people visit the Russian Arctic National Park each year. The Russian Arctic is close to some parts of China, and for the Chinese there are few obstacles to Russian tourism travel. Thirty percent of Russian Arctic visitors come from China (17 percent are from Germany, and only 5 percent are Russians). Alaska sees over 2 million visitors per year (although only about 1 percent of the total direct visitor spending occurred in the Arctic area in Alaska). The number of Chinese tourists including the Taiwanese has increased greatly in recent years, at least until the 2020 pandemic. Fairbanks is a major destination. Before the pandemic, the number of Iceland's tourists skyrocketed to almost 2 million per year. Tourism to Canada, especially from China and Japan, has grown in recent years, and yet the number is small compared to other Arctic nations that market their Arctic adventures extensively and when compared to non-Arctic parts of Canada. Nevertheless, the Yukon Territory receives about 200,000 visitors and Nunavut about 170,000 annually.

This chapter has addressed the question "What is the Arctic?"—looking to its history, its boundaries as variously defined, its peoples (what is common to them, what is not), its political divisions, and its physical and social conditions. What is the Arctic of the future? We turn to that question in the following chapter. Changes in the region are rapid, remarkable and significant, and are ongoing in populations, lifestyles, health and economic patterns, climate, temperature, precipitation, air quality, sea level, biodiversity and species health and movements. These need to be understood to address sustainability of the region. In Chapter 3, we describe in detail the important conditions in the Arctic as well as the leading changes predicted in them. In this new world, Arctic peoples, those who live there, those who make rules for it, invest in it and who do business and visit it, act in ways that can sustain the physical environment and traditional lifestyles, or hurt both.

NOTES

1 Personal interview with Canadian official involved in Indigenous and Northern Affairs, Canada, July 24, 2018.

2 Koovian Flanagan, a senior advisor, Inuit Community Relations, hosted me in a most informative and generous way during my visit to Nunavut.

3 Jerry Ell was a renowned artist and carver, who passed away from cancer in January 2020.

4 Jerry did not say more about the schools, a subject we address in Chapter 2.

5 Arctic art collections are found in many places. See "Norwegian Artists Paint the Arctic," The Norwegian American, accessed June 13, 2020, last updated December 26, 2020, https://www.norwegianamerican.com/norwegian-artists-paint-the-arctic/; "Museum Catalogue: Kamchatka Catalogue," Scott Polar Research Institute, University of Cambridge, accessed June 13, 2020, https://www.spri.cam.ac.uk/museum/catalogue/kamchatka/browse/.

6 Diana Donald, "The Arctic Fantasies of Edwin Landseer and Briton Riviere: Polar Bears, Wilderness and Notions of the Sublime," *Tate Papers*, No.13 (Spring 2010), accessed 8 January 2022, https://www.tate.org.uk/research/publications/tate-papers/13/arctic-fantasies-of-edwin-landseer-and-briton-riviere-polar-bears-wilderness-and-notions-of-the-sublime.

7 "Northwest Passage," History.com, last updated March 3, 2021, https://www.history.com/topics/exploration/northwest-passage. See also Brenden Rensink, "'If a Passage Could Be Found': The Power of Myth (and Money) in North American Exploration," *Dissertations, Theses, & Student Research, Department of History*. 38, accessed January 13, 2022, https://digitalcommons.unl.edu/historydiss/38?utm_source=digitalcommons.unl.edu%2Fhistorydiss%2F38&utm_medium=PDF&utm_campaign=PDFCoverPages.

8 Mary Wollstonecraft (Godwin) Shelley, *Frankenstein; or, the Modern Prometheus*, Project Gutenberg eBook, last updated November 13, 2020, https://www.gutenberg.org/files/84/84-h/84-h.htm#chap24.

9 Ibid.

10 Shelley Sommer, "Review of *Arctic Disclosures*. Edited by Anka Ryall, Johan Schimanski, and Henning Howlid Wærp," *Arctic, Antarctic and Alpine Research*, Vol. 43, No. 4 (2018): 661–62.

11 "Top 10 Arctic Novels," The Guardian, accessed August 15, 2019, https://www.theguardian.com/books/2016/feb/17/top-10-arctic-novels.

12 Joscelyn Godwin, *ARKTOS, the Polar Myth in Science, Symbolism, and Nazi Survival* (Illinois: Adventures Unlimited Press, 1993), 19, 223.

13 Ibid.

14 Rhodi Lee, "Adolf Hitler's Secret Nazi Base in Arctic Discovered by Russian Scientists," Tech Times, October 24, 2016, accessed August 13, 2019, https://www.techtimes.com/articles/183478/20161024/adolf-hitlers-secret-nazi-base-in-arctic-discovered-by-russian-scientists.htm.

15 Adolf Hitler, Quotes from Mein Kampf, 245, accessed August 13, 2019, https://www.nationalists.org/quotes/mein-kampf.html#aryan/.

16 S. G. Morton, *Crania Americana or, A Comparative View of the Skulls of Various Aboriginal Nations of North and South America* (Philadelphia: Remington, 1839).

17 Derek Kane O'Leary, "The Arctic Other in American Cultural and Intellectual History," The Arctic Institute, August 21, 2018, https://www.thearcticinstitute.org/arctic-other-american-cultural-intellectual-history/.
18 Ibid.
19 Ibid.
20 Eskimo is a term considered pejorative by some, and movements exist to remove its use. But it is also used to self-identify by others.
21 Translated from the Italian: "Per una vacanza indimenticabile per tutta la famiglia e realizzare un sogno per grandi e piccini [...] e che dovrebbero fare almeno una volta nella vita, se non altro per incontrare di persona Babbo Natale."
22 United Nations Department of Economic and Social Affairs, *State of the World's Indigenous Peoples: Education* (Geneva: United Nations, 2017), 62.
23 "Arctic Indigenous Peoples," Arctic Centre, University of Lapland, accessed February 6, 2022, https://www.arcticcentre.org/EN/arcticregion/Arctic-Indigenous-Peoples.
24 Ligaya Mishan, "In the Arctic, Reindeer Are Sustenance and a Sacred Presence," The New York Times Style Magazine, November 17, 2020, https://www.nytimes.com/2020/11/09/t-magazine/reindeer-arctic-food.html, 26.
25 Nymand Larsen, Gail Fondahl and Peter Schweitzer, "Arctic Social Indicators: A Follow-Up to the Arctic Human Development Report," TemaNord (Copenhagen: Nordic Council of Ministers, 2010), http://norden.diva-portal.org/smash/record.jsf?pid=diva2%3A701571&dswid=adScripts:alpha.
26 Eduardo Chachamovich, Laurence Kirmayer, John M. Haggarty, Margaret Cargo, Rod McCormick and Gustavo Turecki, "Suicide among Inuit: Results from a Large, Epidemiologically Representative Follow-Back Study in Nunavut," *Canadian Journal of Psychiatry*, Vol. 60, No. 6 (June 2015), https://ncbi.nlm.nih.gov/pmc/articles/pmc4501584.
27 Ibid.
28 Ibid.
29 "Food Security across the Arctic," Inuit Circumpolar Council—Canada (May 2012). See also Evan Lubofsky, "Hunger in the Arctic Prompts Focus on Causes, Not Symptoms," Woods Hole Oceanic Institution, November 5, 2020, accessed August 20, 2021, https://www.whoi.edu/news-insights/content/hunger-in-the-arctic-prompts-focus-on-causes-not-symptoms/.https://www.whoi.edu/news-insights/content/hunger-in-the-arctic-prompts-focus-on-causes-not-symptoms/.
30 Elyse Skura, "Food in Nunavut Still Costs up to 3 Times National Average," CBC News, June 24, 2016, accessed August 11, 2021, https://www.cbc.ca/news/canada/north/nunavut-food-price-survey-2016-1.3650637.
31 G. F. Romashkina, V. A. Davydenko1 and R. R. Khuziakhmetov, "Problems of Food Security in the Russian Arctic," *IOP Conference Series: Materials Science and Engineering*, Vol. 940 (October 2020), accessed August 11, 2021, https://iopscience.iop.org/article/10.1088/1757-899X/940/1/012122/meta.
32 "Developing Oil and Gas Resources in Arctic Waters: The Final Frontier?," accessed September 2, 2020, http://library.arcticportal.org/1919.
33 Birger Poppel, "Arctic Oil & Gas Development: The Case of Greenland," *Arctic Yearbook 2018* (Akureyri, Iceland: Northern Research Forum, 2018), 328–60.
34 "Greenland in Figures (2020)," Statistics Greenland, May 2020, http://www.stat.gl/publ/en/GF/2020/pdf/Greenland%20in%20Figures%202020.pdf.

35 Interview, KNABK headquarters, Nuuk, June 2019.
36 Interview, Nuuk, June 12, 2019.
37 Karin Kirk, "92% of Greenland's Residents Believe Climate Change Is Happening," Yale Climate Connections, October 17, 2019, accessed July 16, 2020, https://yaleclimateconnections.org/2019/10/92-percent-of-greenlands-residents-believe-climate-change-is-happening/. The study quoted was by K. Minor, G. Agneman, N. Davidsen, N. Kleemann, U. Markussen, A. Olsen, D. Lassen, and M. T. Rosing, "Greenlandic Perspectives on Climate Change: 2018–2019 Results from National Survey" (2019), University of Greenland and University of Copenhagen, Kraks Fond Institute for Urban Research, accessed February 6, 2022, https://www.researchgate.net/publication/339177908_Greenlandic_Perspectives_on_Climate_Change_2018-2019_Results_from_a_National_Survey.
38 Kirk,"92% of Greenland's Residents Believe Climate Change Is Happening."
39 Meilan Solly, "Straight from a Greenland Fjord, London Installation Sends Dire Message on Climate Change," Smithsonian Magazine, December 12, 2018.
40 Elizabeth Kolbert, "Greenland Is Melting," *New Yorker*, Vol. 92, No. 34 (October 24, 2016): 50–61, https://www.newyorker.com/magazine/2016/10/24/greenland-is-melting.
41 Michael Pye, "Small but Mighty," *The New York Times Book Review*, June 6, 2021, 42.
42 "Iceland," The Arctic Institute, https://www.thearcticinstitute.org/countries/iceland/.
43 Viðar Helgason, "Iceland Champions the Power of Geothermal Energy for the Environment and Businesses," November 29, 2017, accessed August 3, 2021, https://www.theneweconomy.com/energy/iceland-champions-the-power-of-geothermal-energy-for-the-environment-and-businessesust.
44 "Consequences of Tourism," https://11geokellyluo.weebly.com/tourism-impacts.html.
45 "Iceland," The Arctic Institute.
46 "Arctic Norway," Wikipedia, revised December 13, 2021, accessed February 6, 2022, https://en.wikipedia.org/wiki/Arctic_Norway.
47 Stephanie Pearson, "Norway's Bold Plan to Tackle Overtourism," Outside Magazine, September 3, 2019, https://www.outsideonline.com/2401446/norway-adventure-travel-overtourism.
48 "Norway Wealth Fund Earned a Record $180 Billion in 2019," February 27, 2020, https://www.cnbc.com/2020/02/27/norway-wealth-fund-earned-a-record-180-billion-in-2019.html.
49 "This Is Norway 2019," October 14, 2019, accessed July 16, 2020, https://www.ssb.no/en/befolkning/artikler-og-publikasjoner/this-is-norway-2019.
50 "Key Indicators of Arctic Climate Change 1971–2017," October 12, 2018, https://iopscience.iop.org/article/10.1088/1748-9326/aafc1b/pdf.
51 https://www.regjeringen.no/contentassets/202fec60ac844d4ca7d53d65b6b9ac9c/alle-regjeringa-vil-punkt-i-meldinga.pdf
52 "Norway's Comprehensive Climate Action Plan," Solberg's Government, Ministry of Climate and Environment, August 1, 2021, accessed February 6, 2022, https://www.regjeringen.no/en/aktuelt/heilskapeleg-plan-for-a-na-klimamalet/id2827600/; "Norway's Climate Action Plan" (Meld. St. 13, 2020–21), accessed August 8, 2021 (proposed policies in detail), https://www.regjeringen.no/contentassets/202fec60ac844d4ca7d53d65b6b9ac9c/alle-regjeringa-vil-punkt-i-meldinga.pdf.

53 "World Development Indicators," World Bank Group, accessed February 6, 2022, https://datatopics.worldbank.org/world-development-indicators/.
54 J. P. Casey, "Moving a Town to Save a Mine: The Story of Kiruna," Mining Technology, accessed August 25, 2020, https://www.mining-technology.com/features/moving-a-town-to-save-a-mine-the-story-of-kiruna/.
55 "The Sámi in Finland," Samediggi, accessed July 28, 2020, https://www.samediggi.fi/sami-info/?lang=en.
56 "Far North (Russia)," Wikipedia, last updated January 11, 2022, accessed February 6, 2022, https://en.wikipedia.org/wiki/Far_North_(Russia).
57 In 2019, Yakutsk was connected to the Russian rail network linking it to Moscow by train for the first time. Marlene Laruelle and Sophie Hohmann. "Biography of a Polar City: Population Flows and Urban Identity in Norilsk," *Polar Geography*, Vol. 40, No. 4 (October 2, 2017): 306–23, https://doi.org/10.1080/1088937X.2017.1387822.
58 Ibid.
59 Peter B. Danilov, "Russia Approves Six Major Investment Projects in the Arctic, North High News," February 1, 2021, https://www.highnorthnews.com/en/russia-approves-six-major-investment-projects-arctic. See also Eugene Rumer, Richard Sokolsky and Paul Stronski, "Russia in the Arctic—A Critical Examination," Carnegie Endowment For International Peace, March 29, 2021, accessed August 9, 2021, https://carnegieendowment.org/2021/03/29/russia-in-arctic-critical-examination-pub-84181.
60 Anticipating Chapter 4's Summary of the Inventory of Tools to Address Arctic Sustainability, the Russian government ordered Norilsk Nickel, the responsible company, to pay almost 150 billion rubles (around 2 billion dollars). Olesya Vikulova, "A Year after the Norilsk Disaster, Where Are Russia's Oil Risks and What Needs to be Done?," May 29, 2021, accessed June 24, 2021, https://www.greenpeace.org/international/story/47973/norilsk-oil-spill-disaster-russia-accident-risk-map/.
61 Roland Matthews, "Kursk Submarine Disaster," Britannica, last updated August 5, 2021, accessed June 16, 2020, https://www.britannica.com/event/Kursk-submarine-disaster.
62 "Languages," Alaska Native Language Center, accessed June 24, 2021, https://www.uaf.edu/anlc/languages.php.
63 "QuickFacts: Alaska," US Census Bureau, accessed August 16, 2021, https://www.census.gov/quickfacts/AK.
64 "Alaska Natives," World Directory of Minorities and Indigenous Peoples, Minority Rights Group International, accessed February 6, 2022, https://minorityrights.org/minorities/alaska-natives/.
65 "United States," The Arctic Institute, Center for Circumpolar Security Studies, revised June 19, 2020, accessed February 6, 2022 https://www.thearcticinstitute.org/countries/united-states/.
66 "Changes in the Arctic: Background and Issues for Congress," last updated March 4, 2019, Congressional Research Service, https://crsreports.congress.gov/product/pdf/R/R41153/144.
67 Matthew Berman, "Resource Rents, Universal Basic Income, and Poverty among Alaska's Indigenous Peoples," *World Development*, No. 106 (June 1, 2018): 161–72, https://doi.org/10.1016/j.worlddev.2018.01.014.
68 Mia Bennett, "What Happens to Arctic Tourism when When the Ice Melts?," Journal of the North Atlantic and Arctic (October 5, 2018), accessed February 6, 2022, https://www.jonaa.org/content/2018/10/5/arctic-tourism.

69 In spring of 2021, the Biden administration suspended oil and gas leasing activity in ANWR.

70 Joel Reynolds, "Bristol Bay Tribes to EPA: Veto Pebble Mine Now and Forever," NRDC, June 1, 2021, accessed June 25, 2021, https://www.nrdc.org/experts/joel-reynolds/bristol-bay-tribes-epa-veto-pebble-mine-now-and-forever.

71 Henry Fountain, "A Clash of Buried Treasure and Living Treasure in Alaska," *The New York Times*, July 27, 2020, A-15, cols 1–5.

72 I am indebted to an anonymous reviewer for comments on Pebble Mine.

73 Fountain, "A Clash of Buried Treasure and Living Treasure in Alaska."

74 Robert T. Anderson, "Sovereignty and Subsistence: Native Self-Government and Rights to Hunt, Fish, And Gather After ANSCA," , *Alaska Law Review*, Vol. 33, No. 187 (2016): 187–227.

75 Sally Hardin and Jenny Rowland-Shea, "The Most Powerful Arctic Oil Lobby Group You've Never Heard of, Center for American Progress," accessed August 9, 2021, https://www.americanprogress.org/issues/green/reports/2018/08/09/454309/powerful-arctic-oil-lobby-group-youve-never-heard/. See also Scott Wilson, "ANWR: The Great Divide," Smithsonian Magazine, October 2005, accessed August 9, 2002, https://www.smithsonianmag.com/science-nature/anwr-the-great-divide-69848411/.

76 Mia M. Bennett, "From State-Initiated to Indigenous-Driven Infrastructure: The Inuvialuit and Canada's First Highway to the Arctic Ocean," *World Development*, Vol. 109 (September 2018): 134, https://doi.org/10.1016/j.worlddev.2018.04.003.

77 "Canada," The Arctic Institute, accessed December 20, 2019, https://www.thearcticinstitute.org/countries/canada/.

78 Baron, Marie, Mylène Riva and Christopher Fletcher, "The Social Determinants of Healthy Ageing in the Canadian Arctic," *International Journal of Circumpolar Health*, Vol. 78, No. 1 (January 1, 2019), https://doi.org/10.1080/22423982.2019.1630234.

79 Pamela Y. Collins, Roberto A. Delgado, Beverly A. Pringle, Catherine Roca and Anthony Phillips, "Suicide Prevention in Arctic Indigenous Communities," *The Lancet Psychiatry*, Vol. 4, No. 2 (February 1, 2017): 92–94, https://doi.org/10.1016/S2215-0366(16)30349-2.

80 Joe Sawchuk, "Social Conditions of Indigenous Peoples in Canada," The Canadian Encyclopedia, last updated May 2020, accessed July 28, 2020, https://www.thecanadianencyclopedia.ca/en/article/native-people-social-conditions.

81 Harvey A. Mccue and Michelle Filice, "Education of Indigenous Peoples in Canada," The Canadian Encyclopedia, June 6, 2011, last updated July 18, 2018, accessed July 28, 2020, https://www.thecanadianencyclopedia.ca/en/article/aboriginal-people-education.

82 Minnie Aodla Freeman, Anne-marie Pedersen, Zach Parrott and David Gallant, "Inuit," The Canadian Encyclopedia, June 8, 2010, last updated September 24, 2020, accessed February 6, 2022, https://www.thecanadianencyclopedia.ca/en/article/inuit.; Milton M. R. Freeman, "Arctic Indigenous Peoples in Canada," The Canadian Encyclopedia, last updated October 24, 2017, accessed November 7, 2019, https://www.thecanadianencyclopedia.ca/en/article/aboriginal-people-arctic.

83 "First Peoples" includes Inuit, First Nations (Indians) and Métis. Inuit are "Aboriginal" or "First Peoples," but are not "First Nations," because "First Nations" are Indians.

Inuit are not Indians. "Indigenous Peoples" includes the aboriginal or First Peoples of Canada and other countries. "Indigenous Peoples" is used in an international context, such as in United Nations Declaration of the Rights of Indigenous Peoples. "A Note on Terminology: Inuit, Metis, First Nations, and Aboriginal," Bowmanville Rotary Club, accessed July 17, 2010, https://www.bowmanvillerotaryclub.org/sitepage/a-note-on-terminology-for-indigenous-peoples.

84 Sarah Isabel Wallace, "William Treaties," The Canadian Encyclopedia, last updated April 18, 2018, accessed July 17, 2020, https://www.thecanadianencyclopedia.ca/en/article/williams-treaties.

85 Truth and Reconciliation Commission of Canada, "Honouring the Truth, Reconciling for the Future: Summary of the Final Report of the Truth and Reconciliation Commission of Canada," accessed August 13, 2021, https://irsi.ubc.ca/sites/default/files/inline-files/Executive_Summary_English_Web.pdf.

86 "Until There Is Not a Single Indian in Canada," Facing History & Ourselves, accessed July 29, 2020, https://www.facinghistory.org/stolen-lives-indigenous-peoples-canada-and-indian-residential-schools/historical-background/until-there-not-single-indian-canada.

87 Truth and Reconciliation Commission of Canada, "Honouring the Truth, Reconciling for the Future."

88 Almost three-quarters of Inuit live in Inuit Nunangat, which is the name of the land and surrounding water and ice. Inuit consider the latter two to be part of their way of life. There are more than 65,025 Inuit in Canada (as of 2016), over 30 percent more than in 2006.

89 "China Regional Snapshot: Arctic," 2020 House Foreign Affairs Committee GOP, last updated March 16, 2021, accessed February 6, 2022, https://gop-foreignaffairs.house.gov/china-regional-snapshot-arctic/; Marisa R. Lino, "Understanding China's Arctic Activities," IISS, February 25, 2020, accessed August 2, 2020, https://www.iiss.org/blogs/analysis/2020/02/china-arctic.

90 Martin Breum, "Public Hearings on a Controversial Greenland Mine Get Underway," Arctic Today, December 18, 2020, accessed August 2, 2021, https://www.arctictoday.com/public-hearings-on-a-controversial-greenland-mine-get-underway/.

91 For a five-year study period.

92 According to a ANCAN report, CNA is a nonprofit research and analysis organization that studies domestic policy issues for federal, state and local government agencies (https://www.cna.org).

93 Pat Davis Szymczak, "Extended-Reach Drilling Hits Mainstream to Squeeze Difficult Reservoirs," *Journal of Petroleum Technology*, Vol. 73, No. 08 (August 1, 2021), accessed August 9, 2021, https://jpt.spe.org/extended-reach-drilling-hits-mainstream-to-squeeze-difficult-reservoirs.

94 Peter Danilov, "China Communications Construction Company Got a Contract to Build an LNG Transshipment Terminal in Kamchatka for Novatek." High North News, accessed August 13, 2021, https://www.highnorthnews.com/en/chinese-state-owned-construction-company-got-contract-build-lng-terminal-kamchatka.

3

THE ENVIRONMENT AND HOW IT IS CHANGING

They looked out and he and the sled: nowhere to be seen. How could he be nowhere? He knew the ice so well, [and was] on it every week for almost sixty years. His sled had listed, then tilted. He would right it as he always did, shifting his body out of the seat. He was strong enough to maneuver his Arctic Cat. The sled was now heavy, sinking. The ice cracked loudly, like a terrible amplified bone break, and the black water was coming in, just a small volume at first. Then, an avalanche of almost freezing Arctic water. And he was under [...] He was with Moon Man, or Takanakapsaluk [Sedna] had taken him. Another sadness in Kivalina. No, a tragedy. No, a homicide.

* * *

They no longer knew the ice. Like the great white bears, their experience, their instinct was not enough. The village, its land, shrank too, like the ice—from 55 acres in 1954 to 27 acres fifty years later in 2003. The shoreline was moving; it was crumbling. Houses hanging out in the sea soon would be gone.

* * *

I've never seen a skinny polar bear. Seals like to swim along the shore, back and forth. The polar bears know that. (Jerry from Iqaluit)

* * *

As the permafrost thaws across Yakutia, some land sinks, transforming the terrain into an obstacle course of hummocks and craters—called thermokarst. It can sink further to become swamps, then lakes. From the air, thermokarst looks as if giant warts are plaguing the earth.[1]

* * *

"There might as well have been a war here," said Mr. Makarkov, whose new house is raised off the ground on pillars sunk 16 feet, where there is still

> permafrost. "Soon there will be no flat land left in this village. I only have 30–40 years to live, so hopefully my new house will last that long."[2]
>
> * * *
>
> Instead of the question being "how do we make sure nothing happens in the Arctic?" the question needs to be "how do we advance economic opportunity, support Arctic sovereignty and prosperity and do so in a way that properly balances environmental considerations?"
>
> There is also a desire to preserve the current status, which is a worthy cause that deserves time, energy and funds. However, I also believe that conversations must also be occurring that relate to the evolving environment and how communities will need to adapt. Communities should be allowed to mourn the loss of resources, places and practices due to the changing environment, but they must also look to ways to survive and evolve to ensure they have a continued presence in the Arctic even if it is changed.[3]

To know how well the Arctic is being protected requires understanding its environment now and how its land, the sea and its societies are changing. That "environment" is understood differently than it was at the beginning of the environmental movement. During its early years, both at the country and international levels, the focus of environmentalism was mainly on water, air, species, land, toxics, hazards and pesticides. These concerns still are central. But over the last three decades, the understanding of what the environment is has come to include for many its people: the "human" environment. Now people count seriously: people on their land, people trying to sustain their cultures and ways of living. Of course, for Arctic peoples, this was always their environment.

An early message from an important United Nations document in the story of environment and people *Our Common Future*—or the Bruntland Report in honor of the Norwegian prime minister who was chair of the World Commission on Environment and Development—stated:

> Sustainable development requires meeting the basic needs of all and extending to all the opportunity to satisfy their aspirations for a better life [...] [S]ustainable development requires the promotion of values that encourage consumption standards that are within the bounds of the ecological possible and to which all can reasonably aspire.[4]

Later, another important policy statement of Arctic leaders declared sustainable development has three goals, three integrated pillars: "economic development, social development, and environmental protection."[5] A broader understanding includes sustainability of cultures, which many friends of the Arctic consider critical.

WHOSE SUSTAINABILITY?

Sustaining people, cultures and traditions is completely compatible with protecting the physical environment. Yet, pursuing each of these pillars (or goals or dimensions) can conflict with some classical views of environmental protection. Going beyond the original focus on the environment has opened the door to developments that are aesthetically insulting if not truly physically detrimental. At the same time, these projects (mining, infrastructure, and highways as well as construction of energy facilities) also generate employment and funds to improve education, provide health care, and make daily life more comfortable. But they also can disrupt traditions and lifestyles.[6]

An example of trade-offs among cultural preservation, economic development and environmental protection can be seen in the fascinating story of reindeer herding culture in the European Arctic. Land-use changes challenge the traditions in many ways. Mining in Russia and other parts of the Arctic has led to building more roads and associated development, which has supplanted reindeer grazing areas. Wind power farms, hydropower siting and industrial development also disrupt herd migrations. Now, reindeer losses are rising as attacks of predators on reindeer calves are more common because wolves have been officially protected. Timber production brings economic opportunity such as jobs and taxes to northern Norway, Sweden and Finland, but also destroys or fragments valuable habitation. Logging and related industry activity depletes reindeer pasture and threatens herding activity. There is also the increase in ecotourism associated in part with the lure of seeing reindeer. But tourism is not inherently benign; it is often accompanied by greater noise, land erosion and generation of waste and other pollution. Seasonal workers get recruited to fill jobs, but they can also create greater need for social services. At times, intercultural tensions and other social problems come with temporary employment migration and with boom and bust cycles. Roads, airfields and snow vehicles that move tourists and new workers and their families generate economic growth; but they also change the nature of traditional lifestyles and the Arctic landscape.

THE NEW HARPOON

Some seek economic development—rather than or in addition to environmental protection—in advocating for sustainability in the Arctic. But the links between growth and a positive future for the Arctic are not always positive. Whether they are constructive or not depends in part on the definition of sustainability. Sustainability of culture is a touchstone that distinguishes some Arctic people's goals. For example, in Sweden, the mining boom has been accompanied by an active movement to sustain Sámi identity, called "the final struggle," for the survival of the Sámi culture and its reindeer herding. Younger Sámi look to their elders as transmitters of that culture; they cite the importance of moral support from the elderly—going as far as celebrating older people for their contributions to maintaining traditions on Facebook and Twitter.[7] The Tornedalers, a national minority group in Northern Sweden, exemplifies the role of connection with nature in the context of everyday lives in small rural villages. Here, ways of life based on traditional livelihoods have adapted to nature and climate, and many people want them to continue.[8] The people here value freedom and nature, including quotidian activities of wild berry picking and hunting.

Cultural sustainability may explain some positive health outcomes. The Unangan (called "Aleut" by some), the native people of the Aleutian Islands in Alaska, have a lower suicide incidence than other native peoples. This is believed to stem from having a clear cultural identity, engaging in commercial fishing and practicing their long-held religion, Russian Orthodox.[9] Observers of the community explain:

> Fishing provides […] social rules and aspirations, as well as the economic means to change unfortunate circumstances; Russian Orthodoxy enriches their lives by imbuing them with meaning; and cultural revitalization and social cohesion counter feelings of marginalization, alienation and isolation.

Yet the importance of holding on to tradition can be exaggerated or romanticized. Knowing what is sustaining is not always clear. Again, the reindeer industry is a case in point; this is illustrated by a United Nations project involving Nenets—indigenous peoples of Kolguev, an island in the Russian Barents Sea. A dramatic collapse of the reindeer population occurred in Kolguev in 2013–14. The Nenets lost their main income source, and their indigenous culture was threatened. A shift from nomadic practices to sedentary lifestyles followed. Kolguev's reindeer herders traditionally migrated with their herds, rounding up their reindeer around the tent, called a *chum*, once a day to prevent them from straying too far. In the 1980s and 1990s, the *chums* had been replaced by *balki*, stationary scrap-material shacks that were built along the reindeer migratory routes. To cover the larger distances to the herds, the Nenets increasingly used snowmobiles, a development that was further fueled by the cheap diesel that the oil company ArktikNeft provided. The use of snowmobiles fundamentally changed herding practices by reducing the contact between reindeer and herders. The Nenets grew accustomed to living without reindeer and sought other means of earning a living such as crafting and tourism. Experts working on the UN project considered a return to traditional indigenous practices as sustainable and essential for meeting a scientifically based understanding of carrying capacity. They even organized training sessions for the indigenous peoples to revive traditional practices. But the experts underestimated the power if not the irreversibility of modernization and the unwillingness of the indigenous population to return to previous subsistence practices. While some see this as a loss of traditions, the economic results are welcome by others in the community.[10]

An even more controversial change raising different understandings of what it means to be sustainable involves the history of land ownership and decisions about oil exploitation on land in Alaska. There, after a long series of negotiations over interpretations of the 1959 law that created the state of Alaska and the relative positions of land ownership among native peoples, the federal government, and Alaska, Congress passed the remarkable Alaska Native Claims Settlement Act (introduced in Chapter 2). Under the terms of the law, Alaska's indigenous peoples received millions of acres of land and almost a billion dollars. Finally, the rights and interests of indigenous people in lands they had inhabited for hundreds of years before there was a United States were recognized. This righted at least some of the wrongs associated with ignoring the claims of Alaskan natives about their long-standing interests in the lands, abuse of treaty making and of interpretations of agreements with native peoples. How can this influx of money and land be put to use sustainably? This historical settlement might have been followed by the creation of reservations and encapsulating traditional life ways. Instead, the indigenous peoples started 12 native regional economic development corporations—each associated with the indigenous peoples who lived in various regions of the state.

Perhaps ironically for considerations of what is sustainable development, a major event leading to the agreement under the claims act was the discovery of oil at Prudhoe Bay on the Arctic coast. To move the oil to the Lower 48 states, the oil companies that discovered the rich site proposed building a pipeline across Alaska to the port of Valdez. From there the oil would be shipped to the south. Building of the pipeline, however, required the settlement of the land claims as it would pass over lands involved in the negotiations.

Thus corporate capitalism came to the indigenous peoples of Alaska allowing for economic benefits while sustaining at least some traditional ways of life. Some people were wary as they were concerned about their futures under a corporate model. Business failures could result in the much feared bankruptcy proceedings against these corporations in addition to the loss of hunting and fishing grounds.

But others welcomed the new model: native corporations would be "the new harpoon." A geologist in the region described how the wider world likes to see Eskimos as impoverished and clinging to noble tradition: "This is not a Western [...] The word 'village' has a quaint image that belies the huge dollar cost of these small cities we have built here. This subsistence life style depends on a lot of money."[11] In this view, if oil development in the Arctic is stopped, indigenous peoples will become another type of victim of climate change. "We're selfish about our region," the geologist said. "If we sacrifice ourselves, if we shut down all the Arctic, someone elsewhere will turn the valve open a little more."[12]

CONDITIONS OF THE ENVIRONMENT AND SUSTAINABILITY

Whatever the conclusions about priorities of sustainability goals for the Arctic, understandings of its physical, environmental and human conditions are needed. They help in evaluating the adequacy of environmental rules and how they affect people in the region—some of whom are living very precarious lives. What are those conditions?

Descriptions of the Arctic environment in the *New York Times*, *Sixty Minutes*, *Time*, the *Guardian*, *Le Monde*, *Corriere della Sera*, *Al Jazeera*, *Izvestia* and other important media paint a dreadful picture: permafrost is thawing, sea coasts are eroding, ultraviolet radiation is bombarding people and nature, temperatures are high and destructive, mammals are threatened and the traditional ways of people are under attack. This scene is accurate: some of these phenomena are occurring in some of the Arctic. Where they are occurring, the situation is dramatic and generally serious. But a fuller picture requires responses different from disaster scenarios. Further, although at some level some Arctic conditions are known, much is not known, making strong general statements questionable.

Take the ocean of the Arctic; there is an immense amount to be learned about its health. This is unsurprising because knowledge about all oceans is very limited, and much of the Arctic region is ocean. In 2016, the United Nations published a first comprehensive check of the marine environment. The second report published in 2021 noted only few major changes. The World Ocean Assessment pointed several disturbing trends in the oceans generally and noted large gaps in how the oceans are understood. The report, important to the Arctic even when it is not its direct subject, noted thus:

> The Central Arctic Ocean and the marginal seas such as the Chukchi, East Siberian, Laptev, Kara, White, Greenland, Beaufort, and Bering Seas, Baffin

> Bay and the Canadian Archipelago [...] are among the least-known basins and bodies of water in the world ocean, because of their remoteness, hostile weather, and the multi-year (i.e., perennial) or seasonal ice cover.[13]

What is known led to the conclusion that the oceans off the Arctic nations are generally in good health; they are graded by experts as stable. Greenland, Russia and Canada scored in the low 70s, and Iceland and the United States lagged lightly behind. There is still hope for the oceans, wrote the experts. Scores range from 0 to 100, and a value in 70–80 range would place the area in the top 10 percent compared with similar ocean zones of other countries.

A DOMINANT INFLUENCE: CLIMATE

The story of the Arctic environment is not just that of climate change but because of the power of its dynamics, as for much of the world environment, we begin with it. We start here also because change is the hallmark of climate in the Arctic; it is "on the frontline" of the phenomenon—climate change is occurring here at a pace twice as intense as in other regions in the world.

First, what is climate change? The fundamental dynamics of it are well understood. In brief, the earth is absorbing more heat than it is emitting back into space. This shift often (but not always and not everywhere) has dramatic, destructive effects on people, places and nature.

"Climate is what you expect; weather is what you get." *Climate* refers to both the average and range of weather conditions that occur over an extended period (months, years or centuries). So climate is composed of numerous samples of weather. Deviations from established climate records can occur on a monthly or seasonal basis; they can also occur across longer timescales; for example, warming observed during spring across western North America over the past half century notes an increase in daytime high and low temperatures.

The earth's climate system can be thought of as an elaborate balancing act of energy, water and chemistry through the atmosphere, oceans, ice masses, land surfaces and the biosphere (the parts of Earth where life exists made up of all the ecosystems). These components of climate influence the fate of energy emitted by the sun and received by the earth. Solar energy, or solar *radiation*, serves as the impetus of energy in the earth's climate system. Roughly 30 percent of the solar radiation directed toward the earth is reflected back to space by bright, reflective surfaces, including snow cover, sand and clouds. This same phenomenon keeps a white car much cooler than a black car on a hot day. Emitted energy, or *radiation*, from both the sun and the earth travels in the form of waves that are similar to the waves moving across the surface of a pond. But the energy emitted by the sun and earth is quite different. Each emits radiation at different *wavelengths* (the distance between adjacent crests in the wave) and temperatures. The hot sun emits energy at shorter wavelengths (shortwave radiation, including visible light), and the much cooler earth emits radiation at longer wavelengths (longwave, or thermal, radiation). For the earth to maintain a stable temperature, there must be a balance between the amount of radiation absorbed by the earth and the amount of energy emitted from the earth back to space. The average temperature of the earth's surface in the absence of an atmosphere should be -18°C (0.4°F). But the earth has an atmosphere that traps much of the thermal radiation emitted by the earth's surface while allowing most of the solar radiation to pass through. This acts somewhat like a one-way mirror.

Enter greenhouse gases. Certain trace gases in the earth's atmosphere selectively absorb longer wavelengths of energy emitted by the earth, thereby heating the surrounding atmosphere. This energy is ultimately reflected back to the earth's surface. Hence it has a more difficult time cooling off, and as a result the surface and lower atmosphere warm significantly. Greenhouse gases are a natural component of the earth's atmosphere. Overall, the natural greenhouse effect allows the average surface temperature of the earth to warm from a frigid -18°C (0.4°F) to a more comfortable 15°C (59°F). So, the chemical makeup of the atmosphere helps establish a climate that is hospitable to life.

This description is for the earth as a whole. At local scales, the energy balance equation changes. As a result of the curvature of the earth's surface and the tilt of the earth's axis, the amount of solar radiation received in the tropics is much larger than that received at the poles. But since the rate at which earth emits energy (radiation) to space does not differ as dramatically from the equator to the poles, there is a net loss of energy near the poles and a net gain of energy in the tropics. The ocean and atmosphere transport excess heat from the tropics to the heat-deficient polar regions via winds and ocean currents. Because the atmosphere and oceans redistribute this energy imbalance, much of the earth is livable. The atmosphere responds to unequal heating of the earth's surface by generating atmospheric motion. Atmospheric circulation redistributes heat around the globe in an attempt to create energy balance. Atmospheric circulation responds relatively quickly to radiation. Similar to a sea breeze but a more involved process serves to counter global-scale imbalances in heating: intense surface heating of the tropics creates warm buoyant air that rises to the upper troposphere (the atmosphere's lowest region extending from the earth's surface to a height of about 3.7–6.2 miles or 6–10 kilometers) and moves poleward while cold dense air near the poles sinks to the surface and moves toward the equator. This circulation redistributes energy around the globe thus expanding the livable area on Earth..

Oceans are a key component of climate. Water has a unique ability to store and transport vast quantities of heat. As surface water in the tropics is heated, large-scale ocean currents, driven by atmospheric circulation patterns, transport heat poleward, like the atmosphere's redistribution of energy across the globe, but on much longer timescales. And the ocean also plays a role in determining the chemical composition of the atmosphere: it takes up and releases gases important in establishing the earth's climate, such as carbon dioxide, or CO_2.

The cryosphere is the planet's water that is locked away as ice, including the Greenland and Antarctic ice sheets, sea ice in the Arctic and Southern Ocean, and all other snow- and ice-covered surfaces. Importantly, the cryosphere reflects solar radiation; large ice sheets reflect between 70 and 90 percent of it, allowing very little radiant energy to warm the surface. If the ice sheet were to grow in extent in response to cooling, a greater amount of solar radiation would be reflected back to space, thereby further cooling the planet. But the ice sheet is receding, and so more solar radiation reaches the earth's surface, accelerating the warming of the planet and the melting of the ice sheet.

Greenhouse gases—especially carbon dioxide (CO_2), methane (CH_4), nitrous oxide (N_2O), halocarbons, ozone (O_3) and water vapor (H_2O)—are very effective at absorbing thermal radiation. So, the overall influence is that greenhouse gases warm the planet, making it livable. But, since the Industrial Revolution there have been important increases in the emission of these gases—accumulations due to human activities. They have affected the climate in a way that greatly exceeds those from natural processes, such as solar change and eruptions of volcanos. For example, levels of carbon dioxide have risen from about 280 parts per million in the mid-1800s to about 418 parts per million now. With these changes, air and ocean temperatures are increasing, snow and ice are melting, and sea level on average is rising. Man is altering the climate.[14] The science of climate change has been known for some time. And the percentage of change that is human-caused and can be human-reduced is now understood. Those changes are seen globally, but not in the same way.

CLIMATE CHANGE IN THE ARCTIC

Nowhere is climate change more notable than in the Arctic. In a nutshell, the region is getting warmer, losing ice on sea and land, and losing frozen land. Permafrost is no longer permanent. Arctic rain and snow patterns are shifting.

In places, shores are eroding. The Arctic is losing certain species of animals and plants, and gaining others. It is catching on fire often, and a hole in the sky is opening and closing above it. Its waters are becoming more acidic and polluted in parts, and radioactive in others. Industrial and agricultural chemicals are persistently being circulated throughout it. But the record of environmental change in the Arctic cannot be that simply summarized; here, we lay out the present conditions and changes taking place—not all going in one direction because the Arctic is so vast and varied.

Temperatures

Temperatures have varied in the Arctic over recent decades. In the 1940s, the region experienced a warm period; an update from that time shows continuing annual surface temperature increases. Overall, the Arctic has been warming more than twice, and perhaps three times, as fast as the world as a whole for the past 50 years—and much faster than the average for the Northern Hemisphere.[15] The Arctic warms faster than lower latitudes because darker land and ocean surfaces absorb more solar energy when ice and snow melt: the additional trapped energy increases warming of the atmosphere. Further influencing the warming is the shallower atmosphere in the Arctic compared with lower latitudes, making it less effective in deflecting energy. Finally, soot (black carbon), a significant percentage of which originates in Europe, exacerbates the dynamic.[16]

Alaska, Canada and Central Arctic Russia are warming more than other Arctic regions. The polar parts of Russia have become almost 2.3°C (4.14°F) warmer over the past 30 years. In parts of the region, including the Kara Sea, average air temperatures from 1998 to 2018 were as much as 4.77°C (8.59°F) above normal.[17] In October 2019, the Russian archipelagos of Franz Josepf Land and Severnaya Zemlya experienced the warmest month ever on record. There, average temperatures were up to 8°C (14.4°F) higher than normal. In the winter, temperatures are up to 4°C (7.2°F) warmer in Siberia and the western Canadian Arctic.[18] An update in 2019 confirmed that Arctic warming continues unabated. Arctic annual surface air temperatures in 2014–18 exceeded those of any year since 1900. Over the last half century, in some parts of Alaska, the permafrost temperature has increased to 2.5°C (4.5°F), and in the Bering Sea, recent winters have experienced marine heat waves. In one area of Alaska, the temperature reached 90°F (32°C) for the first time on July 4, 2019. Then in June 2020, the temperature in Verkhoyansk in Siberia hit 100°F (37.8°C).[19] But not all Arctic regions were warmer—a belt of cold weather persisted over parts of northwest Russia and Scandinavia, and Norwegian meteorologists concluded that October 2019 was the coldest in the country since 2009 and 2013. There has also been some cooling in southern Greenland.

Ice

Ice cover is disappearing at a dramatic pace in the Arctic. Shifting and shrinking patterns of white in videos graphically communicate what is happening—creating a sense of doom. Doom is not merited, but concern is. In a 25-year period beginning in 1979, the average period with sea ice cover dropped 10–20 days every decade, and in some areas of the Arctic the drops were much greater. Arctic winter sea ice maximums in 2015, 2016, 2017 and 2018 were at record low levels, and the volume of Arctic sea ice in September 2018 saw a decline by 75 percent since 1979.[20] The US National Oceanic and Atmospheric Administration reported that the 12 lowest extents in the satellite record occurred in the 12 years previous; sea ice has been melting at a rate of 9 percent per decade since the 1970s.[21] There is a lot of variation here: in 2013 and 2014, the ice was relatively higher but still much lower than values in the 1980s and 1990s.

Formerly known as perennial sea ice, melting is affecting some Arctic coastal areas such as in Alaska; ice serves as protection against waves that are driven by winds causing flooding.[22] The Pacific sector of the Arctic Ocean, and Hudson Bay and Baffin Bay experience more open water from August through December. In Alaska, the extent of ice in the summer is about one-tenth of what it was in the 1980s; the Chukchi Sea ice edge in early fall is now regularly hundreds of miles northwest of the Alaska coast. The Bering Sea is a particular area of loss, and the sea ice that does exist tends to be younger, thinner and more susceptible to melting.

An expert made the changes graphic:

> The very old ice that's been around for more than four years used to be 33 percent of the ice cover and now it's 1 percent [...]One way to think about that is, when we look at the area that the old ice covered back in 1985 it was a little bit bigger than the United States east of the Mississippi River. And all that's left now is Maine.[23]

In 2019, Alaska saw the lowest levels of sea ice ever. Mark Serreze, the director of the National Snow and Ice Data Center (NSIDC) said that "if you look at Point Barrow—the northernmost point of Alaska—there's probably no sea ice within 300 to 350 miles right now [...] there should still be some ice close to or along the coast of Alaska, not hundreds of miles away."

Younger and thinner seasonal sea ice leads to the harm or the loss of some species. Other species are expanding their ranges or are present during a longer portion of the year. The expanded open water season (up to three months longer than it was in the 1970s in large areas of the ocean) also promotes shipping, commercial activities, resource development and tourism. The loss of sea ice changes how much heat is in the ocean, which in turn affects fisheries and ecosystems, creating cascading effects. Among people affected are the many indigenous communities in Alaska, including the Inupiat, Central Yupik, Cupik, St. Lawrence Island Yupik and Unangan peoples.

Land-based ice

Land-based ice is also being lost. In the several-decade period beginning in 1971, Arctic land ice loss accounted for almost half of sea level rise during 2003–10, and almost one-third of the total sea level rise since 1992.[24] The Greenland ice sheet is a major source of this rise: on average, it has lost 375 gigatons of ice per year in recent years. To put this in imaginable terms, that is equal to a block of ice measuring 4.6 miles (7.5 kilometers) on all sides or equal to the weight of 2,250 million blue whales. This is about twice the rate of loss from the 2003–8 period.[25] There is some oscillation; for example, in 2017 and 2018, Greenland may have added a small amount of mass.[26]

The degradation of the permafrost

Permafrost is ground that stays frozen for at least two successive years. Permafrost is an important carbon sink, meaning it captures and stores more carbon than it releases, and thus is critical to climate. But, when it thaws, permafrost releases more carbon than it absorbs. Various studies have found that carbon escape from permafrost in the Arctic has been accelerating, although one study found no rise in emissions since 2003.[27] Thawing has now led to what scientists call a positive feedback cycle, whereby an initial disturbance causes effects that return to create some increase in the magnitude of the initial disturbance. Since the 2007–9 period, the near surface permafrost in the High Arctic has warmed by more than 9°F (5°C); also, the layer of the ground that thaws in the summer has deepened. In parts of Alaska, the date of freeze up in the 2010s in the active layer was in mid-December, almost two months later than in the mid-1980s.[28] Also, in Alaska, almost everywhere in the North and in the interior, warming is being experienced at depths of up to 65 feet.[29] The term "alarming" is too often used to describe environmental change in the Arctic, but the adjective does apply here. "Abrupt thaw," as scientists call this process, changes the landscape. It causes landslides. Massive ground slumps have occurred. Forests are affected with flooding, which destabilizes tree trunks and roots. Trees get "drunk": they tip over and are swallowed by new wetlands. People who live in Siberia describe what permafrost loss is like: "There are still little pockets of land, but you have to wade through some pretty wet spots to reach them."[30]

The effect on buildings can be dramatic; in parts of Siberia in the past several decades, the bearing capacity of some foundations has declined by 40–50 percent. In Yakutsk, hundreds of buildings have been damaged as they subside; walking across some city streets can be like traversing moguls. Earth movements sink wooden houses as well as concrete and steel infrastructure in pipelines, airports and factories. And coastal archeological sites rapidly deteriorate. The results are eerie and dark, but their true environmental meaning is a matter of some speculation. Surely lakes will appear and they will be filled with new sediments; thawing will release more climate change gases; and mammoths will again rise, although dead, on the horizon.

Remarkably, some scientists are trying to recreate the mammoth through DNA-based techniques, and some Russians are trying to replace the prehistoric animals with cattle and other surrogates for the beasts in order to slow the thawing. This is geoengineering of a low-tech variety.[31] The imported animals strip the region's dark trees and other vegetation. Grasslands return: they act like a mirror reducing the heat absorbed by the ground—reflecting more sunlight than what they replace. In winter, the newly created landscape allows the freeze to go deeper into the crust, locking carbon dioxide in a thermodynamic vault.[32] A father-son team is working on this idea now. They have brought in Pleistocene-era animals, including bison, reindeer and Siberian horses.[33] Reportedly the temperature of the permafrost can be reduced by almost 9.5°C (almost 15°F) through the work of the species.[34]

Climate change–linked effects

The effects of climate change in the Arctic are large, serious and numerous. Just to offer a few examples: in 2003, 86 percent of 213 Alaskan native villages were affected by flooding or erosion. A few years later, in 2009, the US Army Corps of Engineers identified 178 communities as at risk from erosion alone (flooding was not addressed). That same year, other government reports concluded that many native villages would need to relocate.[35] Houses are falling into the sea, and land mass is shrinking in parts of Alaska. Permafrost thawing undermines infrastructure and also housing in many areas, including in the Russian Arctic. Fisheries catches are less predictable as species move with ocean temperatures. Some marine mammal habitats are degraded. Also, the new environmental conditions are linked to several wildfires in Greenland, including one in 2017 that burned 1,200 hectares of tundra (almost 3,000 acres). The following year, Sweden experienced a heavier than usual wildfire season. In the past half century, the number of wildfires has risen in Canada's Northwest Territories and interior Alaska. In 2019, 2.6 million acres burned in Alaska, leading in June to the first ever dense smoke advisory for particles in Anchorage. Fire managers in the state recently advanced the "start date" for wildfire response from May 1 to April 1.

A description of the Arctic environment based on climate change does not represent the whole picture. Environmental conditions are affected in other ways, some influenced by climate change.

Precipitation

Precipitation is increasing in the Arctic by an estimated 1.5–2 percent per decade.[36] The increase in annual total precipitation from 1971 to 2017 for areas north of 50° N latitude has been greatest in the cold season.[37] And the forms of precipitation are changing. Snow cover continues to decline in the Arctic; its annual duration has dropped by two to four days per decade. In recent years, the June snow area in the North American and Eurasian Arctic has been about half the values observed before 2000. Overall, Arctic spring snow cover extent on land has now decreased by more than 30 percent since 1971.[38] Alaska now becomes half snow covered a week later in October than it used to in the 1990s and the snow is gone almost two weeks earlier than a few decades ago. In Greenland and in the Baltic Sea basin, the loss in snowfall comes with a gain in rain.[39] But this is not constant. In 2018, the snowfall in Northern Greenland was twice as deep as it was in some earlier years, and the snow did not melt until summer's end.[40]

OTHER ATMOSPHERIC CONDITIONS

Ozone

The history of international concern with the environment has focused greatly on the atmosphere. Before the crucial attention to climate change, the worry was about the "hole" in the ozone. There is no hole in the sky, but the term usefully captured the attention of people everywhere because it graphically underscored a threat to plant, animal and human health—a result of the thinning of a protective layer of ozone in the stratosphere. The hole was most dramatically described over Antarctica, but in the Arctic, ultraviolet radiation has also long been a concern. Depletion of ozone over the region has been noted since the early 1980s. For several years, particularly from 1979 to 2000, the spring and yearly average ozone levels declined by 11 percent and 7 percent respectively, and there have been dramatic losses of up to 45 percent. The harmful effects of this change are several. A weakened ozone layer induces cataracts in people and suppresses or destroys the human immune system. It also is a cause of skin cancer. It causes harm to certain species of phytoplankton and disrupts agricultural productivity.

Scientists at the University of California Irvine and elsewhere discovered that the depletion was caused by ozone-depleting substances such as chlorofluorocarbons and (later understood) other chemicals commonly used in refrigerants, air conditioners in homes and automobiles, flame retardants and spray cans including in almost ubiquitous hair products. A worldwide legal ban on the manufacture, use and trade in such substances (described later in the volume) followed.

The status of the recovery of the ozone layer and its permanency in the Arctic is difficult to determine with precision. In the Arctic, "mini" ozone holes develop where, unlike at the South Pole, weather pattern circulations rearrange the ozone. This process can last for as little as a few days.[41] So when the good news of Antarctica arrives (such as in 2019 the South Pole experienced the smallest ozone hole since observations began in 1982) annual variations in the Arctic are much larger, making it hard to confirm whether there has been a definite recovery in the layer since 2000.[42] Anomalies occur: in 2020, NASA and the European Space Agency (ESA) reported the largest hole of its kind ever detected, perhaps related to extreme temperatures and unusual weather during the winter.[43]

Persistent organic pollutants

The Arctic is home to pollution through something called POPs, persistent organic pollutants. These are industrial polychlorinated biphenyls (PCBS), dichlorodiphenyltrichloroethane (DDT), other pesticides such as aldrin, chlordane, dieldrin, endrin, heptachlor, mirex, toxaphene, dioxins and furans. POPs enter the food supply in a number of ways, and some Arctic people are dependent on the marine environment for their diet. Traditional indigenous diets include locally harvested fish, birds and marine mammals. Contaminants that are transported to the Arctic by winds and ocean currents, including some that are now globally banned, pose threats and despite restrictions in use some POPs are no longer declining. By the 1990s, human exposure had reached unhealthy levels.[44] Levels of POPs are high in some Arctic predator species, and other organisms including fish are exposed to significant amounts of mercury and polychlorinated biphenyls. Mercury in polar bears compromises their ability to reproduce; one-third of bears in the Beaufort Sea are at high risk. Their relatives in the Hudson Bay have unhealthy levels of PCB as do killer whales off the coast of northern British Columbia.[45] Killer whales are among the most highly PCB-contaminated species on earth.

The waters

How clean is the Arctic Ocean? Compared to other seas and ocean areas, the Arctic is clean. But there is much that we do not know about it. And there are areas that are polluted in one or more forms. Until recently, ice coverage hindered scientific exploration of the Arctic. Even now, this vast entity is not mapped for pollution in any comprehensive or sizable way. But some things are known: common pollutants are present as is spilled oil. Plastics have entered the Arctic; radioactivity remains; and the waters are becoming more acidic. Acidification is the reduction of the pH of seawater caused by the increased absorption of carbon dioxide from the atmosphere. Arctic acidity levels have been increasing at twice the rate of the Pacific and Atlantic oceans.[46] The change is rapid, but getting a true sense of where and of the stability of the change has been difficult.[47] In some parts of the Arctic, acidification has damaged fisheries.[48] Yields of Norwegian kelp, sea urchins and sea cod, for one, are affected, adding to the effects of ocean warming. Other subsistence fisheries are also damaged.[49]

As in the oceans generally, marine pollution is heavily caused by activity on land. Stain repellants, flame retardants and pharmaceuticals are found in the Arctic.[50] Permafrost thaws and its contents make their way to the ocean. And around the year 2016, people started worrying about plastics in the ocean with the discovery of the massive Great Pacific Garbage patch. The world looked on it with amazement and disgust. That "island" is not in the Arctic, but plastics have made their way into Arctic waters. Compared, for example, with the amounts in the Mediterranean, there is not much now, although abundant concentrations (in a square kilometer [.4 square miles] hundreds of thousands of pieces) are found in Greenland and the Barents Sea. Ocean currents bring plastic there from faraway places. But part of the plastic pollution is homemade.[51]

In some areas, the Arctic is contaminated by radioactive material. Between 1945 and 1980, 520 atmospheric nuclear weapon tests were carried out by the United States, France, China and the then Soviet Union. Dozens originated on the Arctic island of Novaya Zemlya. Their fallout remains. Nuclear waste sunk in the ocean included reactors, waste containers and a submarine. Between 2007 and 2015, radioactive radium-228 concentration grew in the Arctic. Contamination in the forms of thorium isotopes is found in sediments on the massive Arctic continental shelves. Though these levels are currently not threatening, some scientists see them as a sign of negative trends.[52]

BIODIVERSITY

This word entered the world of environmental science in recent years but its definition is shifting and imprecise. Conditions in the Arctic vary with its forms. Overall, the region is less rich in biodiversity than lower regions, and specialists say it is "patchy." By that they mean that the variety of biological resources differs with the subregion. Biodiversity also increases with higher altitudes. Arctic ecosystems are rather young. Still, over 21,000 species of fungi, plants and animals find their homes in the Arctic. And since some Arctic species have survived over the years in extreme conditions, they are quite resilient to environmental change. Added to this strength is the absence of major habit disruptions caused by human activity.

The Arctic is home to three dozen species of marine mammals; the iconic narwhal (called the unicorn of the sea), beluga, bowhead whale, ringed seal, bearded seal, walrus and polar bear live in the Arctic all year round. Spotted seal, ribbon seal, harp seal and hooded seal use sea ice for pupping in the winter and spring. They move in open waters of the Arctic and sub-Arctic during the rest of the year. Many marine mammals depend on ice for at least some of the year: reproduction, molting, resting and feeding require it.[53] Arctic and subarctic regions yield one-tenth of the global commercial fish catch, and subsistence fisheries provide support to Arctic residents. Biodiversity changes in the region are numerous, some quite rapid, as a large volume of scientific research attests.[54] Some of the more notable effects are on large iconic species, on tiny ocean organisms and on forests.

Trees, forests, vegetation

Warming temperatures are changing the landscape of the Arctic. Shrubs are expanding in the tundra: it is becoming greener, and yet in some regions vegetation in the tundra is decreasing. There are more severe fire years. And there are more insect disturbances.[55] Bark beetles are a damaging species. In southcentral Alaska, the area they attacked grew from 33,000 acres in 2015 to 593,000 acres in 2018. Tree lines in northern Sweden have moved higher, up to 80 meters, in the last decades. But not every region has seen this movement. Forest decline has been accelerated in some areas; in other places, forests have "popped up."[56] Despite the increase of vegetation available for grazing in some places, herd populations of caribou and wild reindeer across the Arctic tundra declined by nearly 50 percent in the two-decade period through 2018. Caribou die-offs occur in part because the animals do not have access to food.

Species change: endangered and others

The Red List of the International Union for Conservation of Nature gives information on threatened species worldwide. It includes 13 Arctic or seasonal mammalian inhabitants and 21 Arctic or Arctic-breeding seabirds as threatened species.[57] Eight fish stocks and five Arctic fish species meet the red list criteria.[58] The polar bear and the walrus are "vulnerable," affected by, among other threats, residential and commercial development. The Greenland shark is near to threatened status. But some species are increasing in population, including the humpback whale, the harp seal and the bowhead whale.[59] In the Bering Sea region, ocean primary productivity levels (i.e., algae's actions in changing inorganic carbon into organic things) have at times been 500 percent higher than normal levels. Scientists linked this to the low sea ice extent for the 2017–18 season.[60]

THE FUTURE ARCTIC ENVIRONMENT

That is the Arctic environment today. What is in store for the North in the future? What will our children and grandchildren experience, as inhabitants, or visitors in the Arctic in 10 or 20 or 30 years? As a preface to the scientific consensus, or at least reasonably similar professional views, notable is that individual opinions based on experience show disagreement among experts. Some observers are positive, some very negative, some in between. We asked our expert group whether conditions in the Arctic are improving, deteriorating, or remaining about the same.[61]

The positive or sanguine:

> If species that indigenous people depend upon for food are able to adapt to alternative prey, climate change impacts are likely to be positive in terms of food security.

> This is my personal view—what I have seen during [the] last 40 years in Scandinavia, Russia, Siberia and also a bit in Canada. Life itself has become better and in environment there is a slight difference, but not a lot.
>
> * * *
>
> If you measure by the health and social conditions, the opportunity for a healthy life is better than it was.

Other experts are also hopeful:

> We have not reached a point of no return in the region [...] we're going to move to a seasonally ice-free arctic ocean [...] we can reverse that. But we've got to reverse greenhouse gas emissions. There's no way around that.[62]
>
> Natural selection has been found in experiments to alleviate the effects of severe acidification in just two generations of one species of a [...] crustacean.[63]

Some survey experts are unsure or mixed:

> Conditions are changing and that change is perceived as being bad, as change often is. In reality, we don't know what the long term impacts these changes will have on the environment and society other than they will be changed. Assigning a subjective descriptor (good/bad, improving/deteriorating, etc.) is based on the basic belief that change is bad and ignores that nature is dynamic. I believe that tenet excludes the possibility of considering change as an inevitable component in any living system.
>
> While improvements have been made in discrete areas (POPs, ozone layer protection, contaminated sites management), development pressures are resulting in continued habitat loss for culturally important wildlife populations. Climate change is also resulting in disproportionate effects to arctic ecosystems.
>
> * * *
>
> Nature and environment have always been changing in the Arctic, and whether or not that is good or bad is a question on how you view nature. Nature does not keep status quo. Now if they are man-made, then that is another thing, and that is most likely not good. Some areas and regions will experience the changes in different ways. Some people will benefit from the changes and others will experience the opposite. If animal and plant species are lost, then it is definitely not good.

Some see a bleak future:

> The environment in the Arctic is deteriorating faster than we can protect it and create measures for conservation. The changes in the cryosphere are happening faster than we can manage, and this leaves the environment, and particularly the peoples and the animals of the Arctic, in need of solutions quickly.
>
> * * *
>
> Nobody who lives or works in the Arctic would ask this question.
>
> * * *
>
> Need you ask?
>
> * * *
>
> The northern Bering Sea is in the beginning stages of ecosystem collapse. [Elected officials] Murkowski, Sullivan and Young are oblivious to those facts and are rather advocating for more development which is the reason the world is warming the way that at is. Murkowski, Sullivan and Young see a greater good in exploiting the resources of the Arctic but their and other developers' ideas are toxic ideas [...] directly tied to the problems the Arctic is facing. Indigenous people face destruction from groups such as the Northstar group, the [W]ilson [C]enter, the U.S. Arctic Research Commission, the U.S. Fish and Wildlife Service, the National Marine Fisheries Service, the Arctic Domain Awareness Center, the Center for strategic and international studies, the U.S. Coast Guard and Alaska Native Claims Settlement Act Corporations who desire to develop the Arctic and destroy their own shareholder public.

ESTABLISHED SCENARIOS

Much of the worldwide concern about the Arctic focuses on dire predictions of what can be expected from Anchorage to Alta. Predictions are just that and, with time and new studies, will change. The worst case analysis is dramatic. The best case analysis is unlikely. The most scientifically established scenarios, however, are what Arctic environmental managers must consult. The earlier, and some quite recent, "worst case scenarios" were predictions of the most severe possible outcome that can reasonably be projected for different elements of the environment. Many have already been surpassed. But several other assessments exist, some less pessimistic, for certain Arctic conditions.

Changes cover every aspect of importance to environmental quality and the quality of life of Arctic peoples. They also affect people around the world: how the non-Arctic will adjust, if at all, to global changes in the natural environment. So for helpful action, environmental change must be described without falling into the famous professor story: "on the one hand this; on the other hand [...]." This strong tendency, or professional obligation, led President Truman to wish for a one-armed expert. Striving to that goal, following are the most important findings of a mammoth amount of science. They take into account results filled with a sometimes frustrating amount of uncertainty; conclusions like "standard of living may increase or it may deteriorate; the area may get progressively warmer; on the other hand, areas may get cooler. Overall, activity in the Arctic may capture carbon or it may release carbon."

The worst to best case differences depend on decisions made not only by lawmakers and industry, but also by oil drillers, plastics makers, tourists, motor vehicle drivers as well as people needing air conditioning, heat and protein. If Arctic oil and other fossil fuels are exploited rather than kept in the ground (as is now a rallying cry for many activists), particular types of challenges will arise—and so too will development opportunities. Green economics, green parties, green political movements, renewable energy initiatives and major investments notwithstanding, some continuing fossil fuel extraction in the Arctic is likely. The United States, the Russian Federation, Norway, Greenland and Canada are countries working in various stages of exploration and development. Other non-Arctic nations including Italy have taken steps to drill in the Arctic.

Depending on how things are managed, new oil and gas works will change the environment in different ways. Poorly controlled development pollutes both sea and land. Just as one example, even properly monitored pipelines disrupt tundra areas, from inland to the Arctic shorelines degrading the quality of life of local indigenous cultures by damaging reindeer pastures and disruptions to indigenous lifestyle and other wildlife during construction, maintenance and of course breaks. Exploration and drilling also bring opportunities: directly created jobs, support work of many kinds, including in very poor places in addition to services which can accompany economic growth. In turn, these developments create new polluting activities and bring in people. Some new residents will despoil their adopted communities, while others are dedicated to controlling degradation in the Arctic. So in the next years, what conditions will people likely experience in the Arctic and in the immense parts of the world that it affects?

1. Weather: Temperatures and precipitation

The region will see temperature increases of 2°C (3.6°F) through about 2040. Looking to seasonal changes in fall and winter over the next three decades, temperatures will increase by 7.2°F (4°C)—much more than that projected for the Northern Hemisphere.[64] New record temperatures will be set in some regions. After that, increases may be from around 4°C (7.2°F) to over 7°C (12.6°F) by 2100. Decades long projections are particularly challenging for the Arctic. Some see annual average Arctic temperature increases from +1°C to +9.0°C (+2°F to +19.0°F).[65] The wide range is because predictions come from climate models done with computer simulations using mathematical equations.[66] Precipitation in the Arctic will be different but probably not dramatically so. There are signs of modest increases varying with the region. Also measurements are difficult to make including distinguishing snow and rain in windy areas. More intense storms in the Arctic are not predicted.

2. *Ice and sea level*

Sea level will rise globally. The Arctic is a considerable part of this story. Sea levels rise because warm water expands, but also, and more of a contributor, a warming climate leads to the melting of glaciers and ice sheets. The mass of glacier loss in the Arctic is considerable: Greenland alone has lost over 200 gigatons per year in recent years.[67] In fact, led by the Greenland Ice Sheet, the Arctic accounts for 48 percent of the total global sea level rise that occurred from 1850 to 2000, and 30 percent of the total sea level rise that occurred from 1992 to 2017. Ninety-five percent of the Greenland ice sheet thawed in the 2020 reporting year, coming in part because of an early melt. That same year, Greenland was losing ice seven times faster than it did three decades earlier. The result will be about three additional inches of sea level rise by the end of the century. What's more, Alaskan glaciers contain enough ice to raise sea levels by about 1.5 inches (3.81 centimeters) if all its ice were to melt. And melting it is; nearly 60 billion tons of ice per year have been lost in recent reporting periods. Ninety percent of the state's glaciers are retreating—thinning several feet per year. Other than sea level changes, among the effects are coastal erosion, coastal community damage to buildings and infrastructure, and drinking water contamination. However, changes in the water cycle and melting of ice can provide freshwater to humans and be the basis of hydropower.

The non-Arctic will experience this future. Cities around the world could witness more than six feet (1.829 meters) of flooding by the year 2100. The US National Oceanic and Atmospheric Administration (NOAA) has predicted that sea levels could rise by 10–12 feet (3.048–3.658 m) if global emissions continue unabated. These numbers are averages; some areas would see higher levels and others would be less affected.[68] And there have been indications that the international scientific body, the United Nations Intergovernmental Panel on Climate Change's (IPCC), low-end projections of global sea level rise are underestimated: the Arctic may be largely sea ice free in summer before 2040.[69]

Places most often identified as in danger from sea level rise are Atlantic City, New Jersey; Boston, Massachusetts; Charleston, South Carolina; Guangzhou, China; Houston, Texas; Miami, Florida; Mumbai, India; New Orleans, Louisiana; New York City; Osaka, Japan; Shanghai, China; and Virginia Beach, Virginia. And some islands could be permanently flooded.[70] Countries like Kiribati, Maldives, Tuvalu and the Marshal Islands already are programming to move their people upland or off land. In the United States alone, homes of millions would be inundated. Then there is Bangladesh, which could be swallowed by the sea. Climate experts predict that by 2050, rising sea levels will submerge some 17 percent of the nation's land and displace about 20 million people.[71]

In the Arctic itself, reduced sea ice will improve marine access to the region's riches, expanding opportunities for shipping and possibly for offshore oil extraction and jobs in support businesses. However, the increasing movement of ice can hamper operations. Shipping and resource extraction inevitably will hurt elements of the marine habitat and disrupt some parts of traditional lifestyles.

3. The air, atmosphere

Ultraviolet radiation levels on earth will remain high because of climate change's contribution to the ozone hole. Black carbon in the Arctic will be more common. Black carbon is formed from incomplete fuel combustion such as in diesel engines, wood burning stoves and in wildfires.[72] We see it as soot. When the soot lands on snow and ice surfaces in the Arctic, it impedes the ability of the originally white surface to reflect incoming solar radiation; it amplifies the melting of snow and ice cover, and it can accelerate global warming. The presence of POPs will be stabilized and concentrations of several will begin to drop.

4. The waters

Water quality change remains particularly difficult to foresee. Scientists offer a lot of uncertainty about some parts of the damage to the Arctic. "We have some understanding of how any pollution may be carried by sea ice or on the ocean currents which flow around the Arctic Ocean. Even so, we have little understanding of Arctic ecosystem functions."[73] Ocean acidification will be widespread and rapid. All of the Arctic Ocean is vulnerable because colder water absorbs more CO_2 than other water. Notable are acidifying waters in the Barents Sea.[74] Major oil spills are not necessarily more likely in the Arctic than in other seas, but the potential environmental consequences and cost of cleanup are greater. Accidents and spills of diesel and other fuels increase with the number of ships going through a more easily navigated route. The damage in the Arctic is compounded because oil does not degrade in water at 31°F (.56°C).

Threats arise not only from usual dumpings and leaks from ships, but also from one of the devices that is allowing opening of the region itself: the immensely powerful nuclear ice-breaking submarine. Nuclear-powered vessels can have important effects on the area. They can open up the Arctic to new activities and to increased commerce. When safe and controlled, they can be relatively clean. However, when accidents happen, they can be serious. The Russian Federation has made a commitment to building more of these ships; it now has about three dozen—half the size of the US nuclear submarine fleet.

5. *Biodiversity*

Some iconic species may be extirpated from portions of their range within the next 100 years.[75] Reduction in sea ice likely will be devastating to polar bears, some seals and perhaps the walrus. People will be affected because for some these animals are a primary food source. Tree growth in the Arctic will take up carbon dioxide and supply more wood products that generate employment and economic growth. But that expansion will encroach upon the habitat of birds, reindeer, caribou and other species.[76] Biodiversity will see other winners and losers or, more accurately, the advantaged or disadvantaged.

Change in the Arctic, to its many peoples, its seas, wildlife, climate and weather, has been dramatic. And leading predictions indicate it will be greater than in most places on Earth. A number of its outcomes will be highly disruptive, even transformative; others, less dire than in other regions. And certain changes will prove positive to some places and people. The future depends in large part on how well attempts to sustain the Arctic work. We turn to that question now. We review first the law of sustainability and then focus on other social influencers: business and sustainability, the activities of civil society, the policies of governments and the work of the nonprofit sector from philanthropy to education, science and education, social movements, research and civic action.

NOTES

1 https://www.nytimes.com/2019/08/04/world/europe/russia-siberia-yakutia-permafrost-global-warming.html
2 Neil MacFarquhar, "Russian Land of Permafrost and Mammoths Is Thawing," *New York Times*, August 4, 2019, https://www.nytimes.com/2019/08/04/world/europe/russia-siberia-yakutia-permafrost-global-warming.html.
3 Sample Arctic Expert Survey comments. See description of the study in Chapter 1.
4 Our Common Future, Brundtland Commission, 1987, sections 27 and 15. World Commission on Environment and Development, *Our Common Future* (Oxford: Oxford University Press, 1987), https://sustainabledevelopment.un.org/content/documents/5987our-common-future.pdf.
5 Arctic Council's Fairbanks Declaration (2017), May 5, 2011, https://oaarchive.arctic-council.org/handle/11374/1910?show=full.
6 In considerations of the roles of indigenous peoples in an important Arctic organization, described in Chapter 4, reportedly the US opposition to a focus on indigenous concerns was fueled in part by an American environmental protection lobby which equated indigenous rights with undermining US environmental laws including those protecting marine mammals. Elana Wilson and Indra Overland, "Arctic Indigenous Regimes: Indigenous Issues in the Arctic Council and the BEAR," in Olav Schram Stokke and Geir Hønneland (eds.), *International Cooperation and Arctic Governance: Regime Effectiveness and Northern Region Building* (London: Routledge, 2010).
7 Marianna Liliequist, "Elderly Sami and Quality of Life: Creative Strategies Applied by the Elderly within a Swedish Sami Context," in Paivi Naskali, Marjaana Seppänen and Shahnaj Begum (eds.), *Ageing, Wellbeing and Climate Change in the Arctic: An Interdisciplinary Analysis* (London: Routledge, 2015).
8 Tarja Tapio, "'Our Forest': Ageing, Agency and 'Connection with Nature' in Rural Tornedalen, Northern Sweden," in *Ageing, Wellbeing and Climate Change in the Arctic.*
9 Sean R. O'Rourke, Nadine Kochuten, Chantae Kochuten and Katherine L. Reedy, "Cultural Identity, Mental Health, and Suicide Prevention: What Can We Learn from Unangax Culture?," *Arctic Anthropology*, Vol. 55, No. 1 (January 1, 2018): 119–41, https://doi.org/10.3368/aa.55.1.119.
10 Alexey O. Pristupa, Machiel Lamers, Maria Tysiachniouk and Bas Amelung, "Reindeer Herders Without Reindeer. The Challenges of Joint Knowledge Production on Kolguev Island in the Russian Arctic," *Society & Natural Resources*, Vol. 32, No. 3 (March 4, 2019): 338–56, https://doi.org/10.1080/08941920.2018.1505012.
11 Ibid.
12 Whale Hunters of the Warming Arctic note that few Americans are as affected by climate change as Alaska's Inupiat, or as dependent on the fossil-fuel economy. Letter from Alaska, September 12, 2016 Issue, by Tom Kizzia, September 5, 2016, last accessed February 9, 2022, https://www.newyorker.com/magazine/2016/09/12/fossil-fuels-and-climate-change-in-point-hope-alaska.
13 Jake Rice et al., "Chapter 36G. Arctic Ocean," in *Arctic Biodiversity* (Geneva: United Nations, 2016), https://www.un.org/Depts/los/global_reporting/WOA_RPROC/Chapter_36G.pdf; United Nations, *The Second World Ocean Assessment: World Ocean Assessment II* (New York: United Nations, 2021), accessed May 26, 2021,

https://www.un.org/regularprocess/sites/www.un.org.regularprocess/files/2011859-e-woa-ii-vol-ii.pdf. This article reflects those few substantive additions to understanding of the Arctic from volume I (https://www.un.org/regularprocess/sites/www.un.org.regularprocess/files/2011859-e-woa-ii-vol-i.pdf, accessed May 26, 2021).

14 Joseph F. C. DiMento and Pamela Doughman, eds., *Climate Change: What It Means for Us, Our Children, and Our Grandchildren*, 2nd ed. (Cambridge, MA: MIT Press, 2014); John T. Abatzoglou, Joseph F. C. DiMento, Pamela Doughman and Stefano Nespor, "A Primer on Global Climate-Change Science," in Ibid.

15 Arctic Monitoring and Assessment Programme, "Arctic Climate Change Update 2019: An Update to Key Findings of Snow, Water, Ice and Permafrost in the Arctic (Swipa) 2017" (Tromsø: AMAP, 2019), accessed August 30, 2021, https://www.amap.no/documents/doc/amap-climate-change-update-2019/.

16 "Arctic Centre Factsheets, Climate Change in the Arctic," Arctic Centre, University of Lapland, (2014). https://www.arcticcentre.org/EN/arcticregion/Factsheets.

17 Atle Staalesen, "Arctic Islands 8 Degrees Warmer Than Normal," The Barents Observer, November 4, 2019, https://thebarentsobserver.com/en/2019/11/arctic-islands-8-degrees-warmer-norma.

18 Arctic Monitoring and Assessment Programme, "Arctic Climate Impact Assessment (ACIA)" (Tromsø: AMAP, 2019), 992.

19 Anton Troianovski, "A Historic Heatwave Roasts Siberia," *New York Times*, June 25, 2020, https://www.nytimes.com/2020/06/25/world/europe/siberia-heat-wave-climate-change.html.

20 Arctic Monitoring and Assessment Programme, "Arctic Climate Impact Assessment."

21 "Arctic Report Card: Update for 2018," Arctic Program, https://arctic.noaa.gov/Report-Card/Report-Card-2018.

22 "The Big Melt: Global Warming and Sea Ice in the Arctic," Ocean Health Index, August 2, 2013, http://www.oceanhealthindex.org/news/The_Big_Melt.

23 "Marine Conservation Worldwide," accessed August 26, 2020, https://www.facebook.com/pg/iceladyus/posts/.

24 Jason E. Box et al., "Indicators of Arctic Climate Change 1997–2017," *Environmental Research Letters*, Vol. 14 (2019): 045010.

25 Arctic Monitoring and Assessment Programme, "Arctic Climate Change Update 2019."

26 Ibid.

27 Paul Voosen, "Global impacts of thawing Arctic permafrost may be imminent," American Association for the Advancement of Science, October 21, 2019, https://www.sciencemag.org/news/2019/10/global-impacts-thawing-arctic-permafrost-may-be-imminent; Torben Windirsch et al., "Organic Matter Characteristics in a Changing Permafrost Environment: Yukechi Alas Landscape, Central Yakutia," Master's Thesis, Institute of Environmental Sciences and Geography, University of Potsdam, Potsdam, September 2018.

28 Box et al., "Indicators of Arctic Climate Change 1997–2017."

29 Ibid.

30 "Arctic Permafrost Is Thawing: It Could Speed Up Climate Change," National Geographic, August 2019, https://www.nationalgeographic.com/environment/2019/08/arctic-permafrost-is-thawing-it-could-speed-up-climate-change-feature/.

31 Ross Andersen, "Welcome to Pleistocene Park," The Atlantic, April 2017, https://www.theatlantic.com/magazine/archive/2017/04/pleistocene-park/517779/.

32 Ibid.
33 Ibid.
34 Simon Worrall, "We Could Resurrect the Wooly Mammoth: Here's How," National Geographic, July 10, 2019, https://www.nationalgeographic.org/article/we-could-resurrect-woolly-mammoth-heres-how/3rd-grade/.
35 Congressional Research Service, "Changes in the Arctic: Background and Issues for Congress," updated October 12, 2021, accessed January 14, 2022, https://sgp.fas.org/crs/misc/R41153.pdf, R41153, 182.
36 Arctic Monitoring and Assessment Programme, "Arctic Climate Change Update 2019."
37 Box et al., "Indicators of Arctic Climate Change 1997–2017."
38 Ibid.
39 Ibid.
40 Adam Aton, "Extreme Snows in Greenland Caused Ecosystem's 'Reproductive Collapse,'" Scientific American, E&E News, accessed October 16, 2019, https://www.scientificamerican.com/article/extreme-snows-in-greenland-caused-ecosystems-reproductive-collapse/.
41 "Polar Watch An Ozone Hole (Mini) Has Formed over the North Pole and Scandinavia! Ozone Levels Have Dropped to over 50 Dobson Units Below Normal," Severe Weather Europe, November 22, 2019, https://www.severe-weather.eu/global-weather/polar-watch-scandinavia-arctic-ozone-hole-fa/.
42 "Ozone layer is Healing, but Maybe not the Arctic Ozone Hole, UN Says," CBC, Science, last updated November 5, 2018, https://www.cbc.ca/news/technology/ozone-healing-1.4794803.
43 "Unusual Ozone Hole Opens over the Arctic," The European Space Agency, April 6, 2020, http://www.esa.int/Applications/Observing_the_Earth/Copernicus/Sentinel/5P/Unusual_ozone_hole_opens_over_the_Arctic.
44 "Persistent Organic Pollutants: A Global Issue, a Global Response," United States Environmental Protection Agency, (2009). https://www.epa.gov/international-cooperation/persistent-organic-pollutants-global-issue-global-response.
45 Bob Weber, "Report Says Mercury, PCBs Still Threaten Arctic; New Chemicals Emerging," The Canadian Press, October 15, 2018, https://www.ctvnews.ca/sci-tech/report-says-mercury-pcbs-still-threaten-arctic-new-chemicals-emerging-1.4134844.
46 Lisa L. Robbins, Kimberly K. Yates, Richard Feely and Victoria Fabry, "Monitoring and Assessment of Ocean Acidification in the Arctic Ocean—A Scoping Paper: U.S. Geological Survey Open-File Report 2010–1227" (Virginia: US Geological Survey, 2010). See also Di Qi, Liqi Chen, Baoshan Chen, Zhongyong Gao, Wenli Zhong, Richard A. Feely, Leif G. Anderson, Heng Sun, Jianfang Chen, Min Chen, Liyang Zhan, Yuanhui Zhang and Wei-Jun Cai, "Increase in Acidifying Water in the Western Arctic Ocean," *Nature Climate Change*, Vol. 7, No. 3 (February 2017): 195–99, doi:10.1038/nclimate3228.
47 "Arctic Ocean Acidification," National Park Service, 2018, last updated October 28, 2021, accessed January 14, 2022, https://www.nps.gov/articles/oceanacidification.htm.
48 "Press Release: Studies Explore Socio-economic Implications of Ocean Acidification in the Arctic," Arctic Monitoring and Assessment Programme, October 10, 2018, accessed January 14, 2022, https://www.amap.no/documents/download/3057/inline.

49 Arctic Monitoring and Assessment Programme, "Arctic Ocean Acidification Assessment 2018: Summary for Policy-Makers" (Tromsø: AMAP, 2019).
50 Bob Weber, "Report Says Mercury, PCBs Still Threaten Arctic; New Chemicals Emerging," The Canadian Press, October 15, 2018, https://www.ctvnews.ca/sci-tech/report-says-mercury-pcbs-still-threaten-arctic-new-chemicals-emerging-1.4134844.
51 Claudia Halsband and Dorte Herzke, "Plastic Litter in the European Arctic," Science Direct, Vol. 5 (2019): 308–18, accessed August 20, 2020, https://www.sciencedirect.cm.
52 "Global Warming Is Increasing the Radioactivity of the Arctic Ocean," IFLScience, accessed June 2, 2010, https://www.iflscience.com/environment/global-warming-is-increasing-the-radioactivity-of-the-arctic-ocean/.
53 Rice et al., "Chapter 36G. Arctic Ocean"; United Nations, *The Second World Ocean Assessment.* This publication reflects those few substantive additions to understanding of the Arctic from Assessment II (https://www.un.org/regularprocess/sites/www.un.org.regularprocess/files/2011859-e-woa-ii-vol-i.pdf, accessed May 26, 2021).
54 The latest worldwide assessment from the IPCC, its sixth, confirms the changes which scientists have followed in recent years. It was issued in penultimate form just as this book went to press. See "IPCC, 2021: Summary for Policymakers," in V. Masson-Delmotte, P. Zhai, A. Pirani, S. L. Connors, C. Péan, S. Berger, N. Caud, Y. Chen, L. Goldfarb, M. I. Gomis, M. Huang, K. Leitzell, E. Lonnoy, J. B. R. Matthews, T. K. Maycock, T. Waterfield, O. Yelekçi, R. Yu and B. Zhou (eds.), *Climate Change 2021: The Physical Science Basis. Contribution of Working Group I to the Sixth Assessment Report of the Intergovernmental Panel on Climate Change* (Massachusetts: Cambridge University Press, in press). See "Arctic Biodiversity Assessment 2013: Report for Policy Makers (English)," accessed August 10, 2021, https://www.caff.is/assessment-series/229-arctic-biodiversity-assessment-2013-report-for-policy-makers-english; "Arctic Biodiversity under Serious Threat from Climate Change," ScienceDaily, February 14, 2014, accessed August 10, 2022www.sciencedaily.com/releases/2014/02/140214075511.htm; Margherita Valentina Romani, "Governing Arctic High Seas Biodiversity," The Arctic Institute, July 13, 2021, accessed August 10, 2021, https://www.thearcticinstitute.org/governing-arctic-high-seas-biodiversity/; Gloria Dickie, "Arctic Biodiversity at Risk as World Overshoots Climate Planetary Boundary, Mongabay ," April 29, 2021, accessed August 10, 2021, https://news.mongabay.com/2021/04/arctic-biodiversity-at-risk-as-world-overshoots-climate-planetary-boundary/.
55 "Arctic Report Card: Update for 2018."
56 Bryan Walsh, "How Climate Change Is Growing Forests in the Arctic," *Time*, June 4, 2012, accessed June 2, 2020, https://science.time.com/2012/06/04/how-climate-change-is-growing-forests-in-the-arctic.
57 "The IUCN Red List of Protected Species," International Union for Conservation of Nature and Natural Resources, 2012, https://www.iucnredlist.org/search?query=Arctic&searchType=species.
58 See Jørgen S. Christiansen, Catherine W. Mecklenburg and Oleg V. Karamushko, "Arctic Marine Fishes and Their Fisheries in Light of Global Change," *Global Change Biology*, Vol. 20, No. 2 (September 17, 2013), https://doi.org/10.1111/gcb.12395.
59 "The IUCN Red List of Protected Species."

60 "Arctic Report Card: Update for 2018."
61 The survey is described in detail in Chapter 1.
62 Madeline Fitzgerald, "Parts of Alaska Have No Sea Ice for the First Time Ever as Temperatures in the Region Hit Record Highs," *Time*, August 7, 2019, https://time.com/5646168/alaska-sea-ice-melted/.
63 Arctic Monitoring and Assessment Programme, "Arctic Ocean Acidification Assessment 2018."
64 All five of the Arctic Climate Impact Assessment (ACIA) global climate models show, with two different emissions scenarios, about a 2°C temperature rise through about 2040. Post-2040, the models diverge, showing increases from around 4°C to over 7°C by 2100.
65 Congressional Research Service, "Changes in the Arctic."
66 These generate results by inputting information about parts of the climate system and their interactions: the atmosphere, oceans, land surface, snow and ice, and living things.
67 Rebecca Lindsey, "Climate Change: Global Sea Level," Climate.gov, January 25, 2021, https://www.climate.gov/news-features/understanding-climate/climate-change-global-sea-level.
68 Aria Bendix, "7 American Cities That Could Disappear by 2100," Prevention Web, April 3, 2019, https://www.preventionweb.net/news/7-american-cities-could-disappear-2100.
69 Arctic Monitoring and Assessment Programme, *Snow, Water, Ice, Permafrost in the Arctic (SWIPA)* (Tromsø: AMAP, 2017), accessed August 21, 2021, https://www.amap.no/documents/doc/snow-water-ice-and-permafrost-in-the-arctic-swipa-2017/1610.
70 Jaclyn Jeffrey-Wilensky and David Freeman, "Rising Sea Levels Could Swamp Major Cities and Displace Almost 200 Million People, Scientists Say," Mach, May 22, 2019, https://www.nbcnews.com/mach/science/rising-sea-levels-could-swamp-major-cities-displace-almost-200-ncna1008846.
71 Marcin Szczepanski, Frank Sedlar and Jenny Shalant, "Bangladesh: A Country Underwater, a Culture on the Move," Natural Resources Defense Council, Inc., September 13, 2018, https://www.nrdc.org/onearth/bangladesh-country-underwater-culture-move.
72 Tomsk Polytechnic University, "Scientists Discovered Where Black Carbon Comes from in the Arctic in Winter and Summer," American Association for the Advancement of Science (AAAS), February 15, 2019, https://www.eurekalert.org/pub_releases/2019-02/tpu-sdw021519.php.
73 Elizabeth A. Kirk and Raeanne G. Miller, "Offshore Oil & Gas Installations the Arctic, Responding to Uncertainty through Science & Law," Arctic Yearbook 2018, https://arcticyearbook.com/images/yearbook/2018/Scholarly_Papers/15_AY2018_Kirk.pdf.
74 "Arctic Council Cop 25 Side Event on Ocean Acidification Was a Call for Action," Arctic Council," accessed June 30, 2020, https://arctic-council.org/en/news/arctic-council-cop25-side-event-on-ocean-acidification-was-a-call-for-action/.
75 United Nations, *The World Ocean Assessment and World Ocean Assessment, Volume II* (New York: United Nations, 2021), https://www.un.org/regularprocess/sites/www.un.org.regularprocess/files/2011859-e-woa-ii-vol-ii.pdf.
76 "Arctic Report Card: Update for 2018."

4

RULES AND OTHER INFLUENCERS

In the past, there was no need to have new laws about wildlife because Inuit had their maligait [accepted guidelines which need to be followed, natural laws] about wildlife even though they were not written. The present laws about wildlife are not our maligait. The maligait that we follow are not seen because the Inuit piusiq [the way things are] is not visible […] It is a maligait where respect is shown through wanting the bones of the caribou to feel rested. That way we show our gratitude to the animal.[1]

* * *

"Nobody has to like it. But they do have to respect it. It's the law […] I shouldn't have to explain. It's none of their business. It's the law." (Patrick DePoe, an aspirational whale hunter and treasurer of the Makah tribe)[2]

* * *

The village office received the e-mail at 10:00am, 1:00pm D.C. time. "The number of the take has been recalculated based upon public comment required by the federal Administrative Procedures Act."

The boat that had just gone out, with the new hunters of the tribe, needed to return: The quota had been reached.

"Atâta, [Father] what is happening? I am ready," asked the ten-year-old.

"I don't know. It is wrong. We cannot go out today, or tomorrow. They say we are killing too many. They say the animal will not survive if you succeed."

"But Atâta, who are they?"

People who care about sustainability of the Arctic and its environment are not writing on a blank slate. For centuries, indigenous peoples, settlers, lawmakers, activists, educators, scientists, explorers and others have dedicated much of their lives to attempting to keep this region beautiful, clean and pristine and sustainable or making it even more protected. The inventory of their actions through law, science, education, investments, civil society involvement and philanthropy reads like an encyclopedia. What has been done? What is in place? What seems to be working? Where have there been missteps? What more is needed?

We begin with the law. The rules come from many sources.[3] Most people who care about the Arctic's environmental future think that activities on the ground and in the seas should comply with a wide range of general international law, treaties of nations of the world. Then there are treaties with a direct focus on the Arctic or with great relevance to the Arctic environment. Among the rules that matter are the Arctic nations' own federal or national laws: laws within the Arctic countries, those of provinces, states, territories, and cities—relatively unambiguous because they are those of a sovereign country: made by its legislature, enforced by the government, interpreted by the courts. Then there are the laws, rules and practices of indigenous or aboriginal or native peoples not linked to country-specific law-making institutions. There are also important rules that cover a region or a part of the Arctic, such as the marine environment of the Northeast Atlantic or an agreement among some Arctic countries on the protection of a particular fish species or mammal.

And this is just the tip of the iceberg. Agreements, with many different names, number in the hundreds. They include memoranda of understanding (agreements that give the terms of a commitment among parties) and diplomatic letters between a couple or among a few nations or local governments and indigenous peoples in the Arctic. The opinions or decisions of courts or other tribunals which resolve disputes can be influential as well. Included in the rules are not only what international lawyers call "hard law" (treaties and the like), but also "soft law," the declarations and principles made at international meetings such as the United Nations General Assembly, and conferences, or as preliminary statements to later legally binding agreements. Also important are local agreements between or among tribes, governments and businesses.

The overall combination of legal components is like a Russian doll. The layers influence, touch on and cover a region that is not a legally defined place: the Arctic. One summary of rules that target the environment of some or all of the Arctic countries has a list filling 350 pages, and that does not include separate sections on the Law of the Sea, Fisheries, Shipping and Indigenous Peoples, among other topics in a tome that is 1,484 pages long.[4]

A focus on conditions of peoples, the poor and the indigenous leads to a broader investigation of rules and how they touch on people living, at times, very precarious lives. Rules govern the physical environment, the cultural and human environment, sustainability and human rights. They cover health effects as well as—in addition to, and sometimes in tension with—effects on the atmosphere, the water, the land and the wildlife.

How to describe the rules in a way that captures their scale but does not numb with its volume and detail is a challenge. So too is characterizing what they add up to as influencers of the way the Arctic is treated. But conclusions can be reached if wise decisions are to be made about "what more," if any, new rules are necessary. The results of decades of Arctic rulemaking have been good but not remarkably good. They have not been effective for some of what needs to be protected.

For environmental protection in the Arctic, as is true for environmental law throughout the world, there may be too much law. International environmental law is often criticized as being mammoth, with significant numbers of dense rules which are often inconsistent. Lawmakers, regulators and policy people who work in and for the region have overlapping responsibilities; environmental protection is not their only obligation. When there are, as is true often, multiple other goals (national security, cultural preservation, revenue generation and many others), it is unclear which dominates or prevails. The people targeted by all these rules often face daunting requirements. Tasked with having to choose an environmental technology, or set a standard for water purity, or reach an emissions level, or decide if this individual animal can be killed or exported (live or dead), one may feel lost somewhere in that Russian doll when trying to decide which layer must control.

The rules come in various forms—laws, policies, regulations, norms, principles, customs and memoranda—and do not mesh into a coherent, understandable and workable framework. Often they are communicated by or handed down from agencies or organizations that do not coordinate or even interact. They are rarely negotiated in the same institution or at the same time as other rules (say on trade or security or commerce). After all, there is no world legislative entity nor is there an Arctic Parliament, Congress, Diet, Duma or National Assembly. Rules are made in many places, in many different ways; this explains some of the complications that arise when addressing how useful they are. Treaties require that thousands of specialists come together over many years—culminating only if they are ratified by hundreds of political people. And these are not the same people who need to make the rules work on the ground and in the seas.

Custom, known as customary international law, is part of international law. It evolves in ways that are fairly obtuse—unknowable to many citizens. A concept that is at first somewhat difficult to grasp, it is the law recognized by the international community including by the World Court, which recognizes it as an important source of law. Customary international law is that law of the practices of countries that courts consider when those practices are recognized as legally binding by countries—not just done out of goodwill or as best diplomacy. It is true law, but not law that was legislated, drafted or debated in any single venue.

Norms are shared statements about the way people behave in relationship to each other, often over long periods of time. Yet when a norm exists is not always clear because sometimes only a percentage of people for whom they supposedly apply respect them. Also relevant are specific agreements, memorandum and letters that are drafted, redrafted, approved and sent—often not codified or printed anywhere. Yet their adopters feel bound by them. Most citizens do not know they exist. There are indigenous laws, sometimes summarized, but their authority is at times only in the minds and decisions of elders.

Making some of the rules known is difficult in the Arctic, more so than in some other regions. "Extreme temperatures, vast distances, and widely dispersed patterns of settlement have made it impossible for bureaucracies based in far-off capitals to erect and maintain the kind of infrastructure and institutions that they have built elsewhere."[5] There are no roads to many settled places in the Far North. Flights to Nuuk, Greenland or Dikson, the Russian Federation, might be delayed for days. Fog, wind or blinding snow may force patient would-be travelers to sit in cold, limited airports for hours or longer. Getting people from remote villages to attend meetings or testify can cost thousands of dollars. Electronic communication is spotty or absent in parts of the Arctic. In the Russian Federation alone, there are 11 time zones; a worker in a Baltic oblast (a Russian administrative region) may be arriving at work as a colleague in the Far East is leaving.

To try to present the law on the environmental quality of the Arctic and its sustainability risks being overinclusive, underinclusive, short on specifics or much too long on detail. There is so much. And what is included, what counts, is not a matter of agreement among Arctic followers either within or outside of the region. Where should the line be drawn on what the governing mechanisms of the Arctic environment are? In some ways, this is a version of the challenge to the question: "What is law?" But there are several major agreed upon components. It is visually useful to lay out some of the inventory of rules that apply to sustainability of the Arctic (as shown in Table 4.1). Although an incomplete list, they are important because of the centrality of their goals to sustainability and because all or most Arctic countries have formally committed to complying with them.

The United Nations Convention on the Law of the Sea (for short, UNCLOS), the "constitution" for the seas, is fundamental. The treaty was negotiated over decades. It has 17 parts, 9 annexes and 320 articles. Its hundreds

Table 4.1 International Law that Applies to the Arctic—By media

The font or symbol indicates the main media that is the subject of the rule: *biological*, water, *ocean*, **atmospheric**, mixed*, other**, procedures***.

- *United Nations Law of the Sea (UNCLOS)*
- *Agreement for the Implementation of the Provisions of the Convention on the Law of the Sea.*[a]
- Convention on the Control of Transboundary Movements of Hazardous Wastes and Their Disposal (Basel Convention)**
- Convention on Fishing and Conservation of Living Resources of the High Seas*
- The Convention on Wetlands of International Importance, especially as Waterfowl Habitat (RAMSAR Convention)*
- *Convention on International Trade in Endangered Species (CITES)*
- *International Convention for the Regulation of Whaling*
- **International Convention on Persistent Organic Pollutants (POPS)**
- Global Programme of Action for the Protection of the Marine Environment from Land-Based Activities**
- *The Agreement on the Conservation of Polar Bears*
- Convention on the Prevention of Marine Pollution by Dumping of Wastes and Other Matter (The London Convention)*
- **The UN Framework Convention on Climate Change (UNFCC)**
- **The Kyoto Protocol to the United National Framework Convention on Climate Change**
- **The Paris Agreement**
- *The International Convention for the Prevention of Pollution from Ships (MARPOL)*
- The 1990 International Convention on Oil Pollution Preparedness, Response and Co-operation**
- The Convention on the Conservation on Migratory Species of Wild Animals (Bonn Convention)**
- *The Convention on the Conservation of European Wildlife and Natural Habitats (Bern Convention)*
- *The Convention on Biological Diversity*
- The Espoo Convention on Environmental Impact Assessment***
- **Convention on Long-range Transboundary Air Pollution**
- **The Montreal Protocol on Substances That Deplete the Ozone Layer**
- Convention on Environmental Impact Assessment in a Transboundary Context***
- Convention on the Protection and Use of Transboundary Watercourses and International Lakes
- Convention on the Transboundary Effects of Industrial Accidents*
- Convention on Access to Information, Public Participation in Decision-Making and Access to Justice in Environmental Matters***
- The Convention for the Protection of the World Cultural and Natural Heritage.**

Note:

[a] United Nations General Assembly, A/Conf. 164/37, "Relating to the Conservation and Management of Straddling Stocks and Highly Migratory Fish Stocks," July 24–August 4, 1995, https://www.un.org/depts/los/convention_agreements/texts/fish_stocks_agreement/CONF164_37.htm.

of pages include many policies that directly address environmental quality and many that are relevant to achieving and maintaining it. UNCLOS directs sovereign activities of Arctic states in the ocean. Sovereign means within the exclusive control of the coastal nation, and so the treaty lays out the extent of a nation's control in the seas. UNCLOS governs activities of all countries that agreed to it. One hundred and sixty-eight parties have ratified it, including all of the Arctic states except the United States. The United States follows the main provisions of the treaty as customary international law, but a few members of the US Senate have opposed ratification of the treaty, seeing it as a socialistic scheme and one that infringes on US sovereignty.

UNCLOS "zones" the oceans. Nations have agreed to create demarcations of the waters, regulating what can be done and by which countries within each of these limited areas. Varying amounts of control, or sovereignty, exist in the zones, and each of these areas is named: from the internal waters to the high seas. UNCLOS is central to the way the world protects or fails to protect the Arctic.

As one moves out from a country's shoreline, the degree of authority or control that a country has decreases to the point that it has none. The idea is nicely laid out in the Figure 4.1.

In the internal waters, states have complete sovereignty except for limitations created by other treaties or obligations existing under customary international law. So, because activities on land and in waters that flow to the Arctic affect the Arctic environment, the strength of individual country's environmental protection of its own waters is crucial to overall Arctic environmental quality. Most Arctic nations have strong national environmental laws as well as good enforcement and records of compliance with these laws. There is some variability depending on the category of protection, such as for biodiversity, conservation of natural resources and control of black carbon (which is a strong contributor to climate change formed when combustion of fuels and organic material is incomplete).

Next comes the territorial seas. These extend 12 nautical miles, measured from "baselines" determined in ways laid out in the treaty; they may be straight lines or other forms depending on the nature of a country's shoreline, its islands and reefs. They are fixed to begin at the coast's low-water line. Here, ships have the right of innocent passage and of transit passage. But here also, again of relevance to the environment, the coastal state (Iceland, Norway, etc.) acts to conserve living resources in the zone. It has authority to prevent violations of its fishing rules, and, generally, to preserve the environment and control pollution in that part of the sea. The territorial waters are followed by the Contiguous

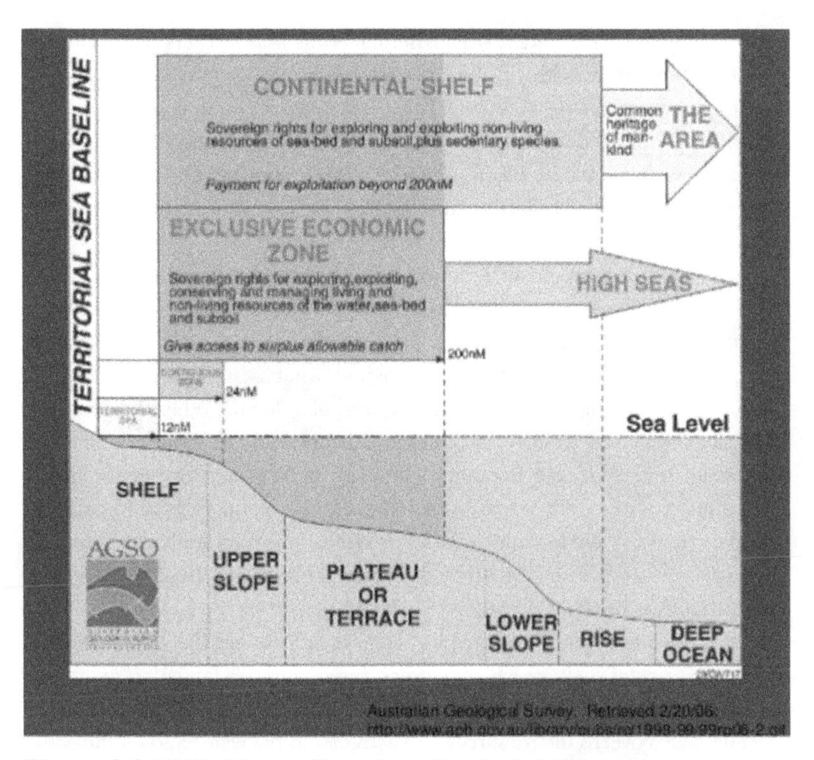

Figure 4.1 UNCLOS zones (*Source*: Australian Geological Survey)

Zones, extending 12 to 24 nautical miles measured from the baseline. In this zone, the coastal state can regulate many activities, including management of wastes. The UNCLOS language includes "prevent infringement of its [...] sanitary laws."[6]

Beyond these areas are the Exclusive Economic Zone (EEZ) and the continental shelf. They can be roughly the same size but the rules for each differ. The continental shelf can reach far into the sea. It has been called a major land grab by the coastal nations: now, through law, they have significant authority in parts of the ocean where formerly there was competition. The continental shelf extends along the natural prolongation (extension) of a country's land to the outer edge of the continental margin or 200 miles—or more in some circumstances. Here, the coastal state has the rights to explore and exploit the nonliving natural resources, sedentary species as well as the activities of the seabed and subsoil under the ocean. Oysters, clams and mussels are among sedentary species: those that are in "constant physical contact with the sea bed." Countries have fought over whether crabs and lobsters are included.[7] Coastal states share with the international community part of the revenue that comes from taking resources from any part of their continental shelf beyond 200 miles.[8] This scheme is the result of a compromise among countries as to what noncoastal states deserve in this extra portion of the continental shelf. The actual collection and distribution of monies is left to the states themselves.[9]

The wealth associated with where oceanic boundaries are drawn can be extraordinary. These boundaries determine which country gets to decide the rules in the zone and how well the resources in that area are protected. Establishing boundaries fairly is challenging: what is just? What practically should be done when coastlines are of irregular form? Where neighboring countries have either concave or convex coastlines, where should the line be? Should inland, land-locked countries have a say in protecting the Arctic? In one boundary case, *North Sea Continental Shelf*, Denmark, the Federal Republic of Germany and the Netherlands asked the World Court to apply the principles and rules of international law that determine boundaries. In 1969, the court found that the countries themselves needed to agree to the boundary lines in accordance with "equitable principles" so as to leave to each country the areas of the continental shelf which constituted the natural prolongation of its land territory under the sea.[10]

The EEZ governs the resources and activities in the water and on the ocean surface. It can extend 200 nautical miles from the shore. Here, the coastal nation has authority to conserve and manage natural resources, both living and nonliving, and to protect the marine environment. The coastal state can exploit or conserve any resources found within the water, on the sea floor or under the sea floor's subsoil. These resources include fish, oil and natural gas. Land-locked and geographically disadvantaged states can take some of the surplus of the living resources of this zone of the coastal states in their region. Coastal states may manage treatment of marine mammals more strictly than the requirements noted in the treaty.

Fish do not have citizenship nor need passports, so rules under the Law of the Sea direct countries to cooperate to protect those fish which come and go in their waters.[11] Migratory species, fish that cross zones, are given special protection.[12] UNCLOS recognizes that coastal states are limited in what they can do to protect these moving animals. It defines which fish fall into this category. The treaty instructs nations to work together to develop programs to limit the excessive take of these species, which include tunas, sharks, swordfish and billfish. Marine mammals are also given special consideration.

The "high seas" are the waters beyond the UNCLOS zones. In the Arctic, there are little bits of what are called areas beyond national jurisdiction, about 1.1 million square miles, the main part of which is sometimes known as the "Arctic donut hole." Is this an area of "no man's land," of no regulations, no environmental controls? Over the centuries of international commerce, no matter how delimited, leading thinkers, such as the Dutch international law pioneer Hugo Grotius, noted that the high seas were open to all and that coastal states could not take the resources for their exclusive use. The concerns that were raised by the countervailing view—that open seas lead to overuse and conflict—have been for the most part addressed by modern rules. Yet conflicts persist. No law is in place that all nations agree controls in these important areas: the surface of the sea, the water below it and the bed of the sea. But they are not open territory because there are other rules which cover them. Take the important topic of fisheries. Now plentiful, Arctic fisheries help feed the world. But if the Arctic continues to lose its ice cover, the growing world population and the insatiable appetite for fish might see a rush to the fisheries of the North High Seas. Here, some cooperative agreements exist such as the Code of Conduct for Responsible Fisheries of the Food and Agricultural Organization of the United Nations, a number of General Assembly resolutions and, as described later, a landmark several year-long agreement to prevent unregulated fishing in the Central Arctic Ocean. And many regional organizations have been established to regulate fishing in the high seas. They set quotas of the amount of fish that can be caught and then divide this "total allowable catch" among states.

Fisheries are also depleted by technologies that can move through the waters taking up targeted fish but also massive amounts of other marine life, including marine mammals and seabirds—killing much that will never be eaten. The United Nations General Assembly in 1994 introduced a global ban on high seas drift netting, a device as long as 20 kilometers (over 12 miles) that can entangle and destroy everything in its path. This is an international step toward limiting bycatch.

Over- or unregulated fishing is not the only activity that can damage the environment in the high seas. The deliberate dumping of toxic and hazardous materials, the nondeliberate spilling of oils and poorly controlled mining activities also threaten the environmental quality of the Arctic Ocean. Environmental rules of individual countries guide how clean or green Arctic mining is done on land. But there is also mining at sea.

In 1868, in the Arctic Ocean of Siberia, potentially valuable metallic nodules were discovered. Since then they have been found throughout the world's oceans. This obscure thing, a fist-sized lump of manganese, was made famous by a Swedish Maltese diplomat Arvid Pardo. In a speech at the United Nations in 1967, he described their potential immense economic value. He also focused on rules to ensure peace in the oceans and to prevent pollution, and called for an international strategy to manage ocean resources. His views became the basis for the notion of the "common heritage of mankind" which later influenced sections of UNCLOS: it holds that certain riches that are found in the seas are owned by mankind as a whole and should be shared in ways that benefit not only the rich but also poorer nations.

A rush, a gold rush, to the seas to take out these minerals and the immense oil and gas reserves in the Arctic has not happened yet; but should it occur the possible environmental effects are numerous.[13] UNCLOS created the International Seabed Authority, based in Jamaica, to manage the eventual exploitation of some areas of the high seas seabed. Its activities reflect a compromise among nations that advocated a sharing of resources and those—most vociferously the United States—that strongly opposed it. "No international organization owns the seas" was among the milder attacks on the International Seabed Authority.[14] Some in the US Congress saw the common heritage notion as a wealth distribution system—communist or socialist.

The general idea of common heritage is now reflected in the work of the International Seabed Authority. The authority has a twofold objective: develop deep-sea minerals and protect the environment. The resources of the common heritage of mankind are owned by mankind as a whole (in the words of international law.) The authority creates policies for the seabed and contracts with private and public corporations to explore and later mine areas of the deep seabed.

The Law of the Sea also covers general environmental protection parts.[15] The countries of the world must work, individually or together, to control pollution from ships, activities on land, the exploitation of the seabed and dumping. Countries also need to protect and preserve rare or fragile ecosystems and the habitat of endangered and other marine life. The treaty requires the use of the "best practicable means"[16] available to achieve these goals.

Under UNCLOS, the coastal states in the Arctic have additional powers in ice-covered areas.[17] Severe climatic conditions create exceptional hazards in these parts of the world. Recognizing this, UNCLOS gives coastal states some more authority, such as over ocean-going vessels.

A number of popular and journalistic accounts describe the Arctic as a place of conflict—especially involving the Russian Federation. International relations between Russia and the West including Arctic nations did chill after the Ukraine incident in 2014 when the Russian military made incursions into

Ukrainian territory and later annexed Crimea. But the Arctic has not been part of a new Cold war; on the contrary, at least until recently, it has been a place of remarkable cooperative efforts. And despite tensions in the administrations of Presidents Trump and Putin, cooperation continues at other levels, among scientists and even diplomats. Differences over territorial control (which nation is sovereign in an offshore place), for example, have been resolved often harmoniously and even with celebration. In the Arctic, there have been surprisingly few disputes. An important potential point of tension existed between Norway and Russia in the Novaya Zemlya archipelago (Russia) and the Svalbard archipelago (Norway), but it was peacefully resolved in 2010. In the Bering Sea, the United States and Russia have worked out a negotiated maritime boundary of 1,000 nautical miles laying out fishing zones and rights. The Russian Duma has not yet ratified the agreement, but the boundaries appear to be respected. There are a few other places of possible contention that can determine how the environment is eventually treated. One involves the tiny Hans Island. Both Denmark and Canada claim the island, an uninhabited barren half square mile dot east of Greenland but also off Canada in the Nares Strait. Even this disagreement will be easily resolved—perhaps simply with a Solomon solution of dividing it in two. Passions behind the dispute are limited: when Canadian military occasionally visit the speck of land, they leave a bottle of Canadian Club; when the Danes do, they drop off a bottle of schnapps with a welcome to Denmark sign.[18]

Under the leadership of Vladimir Putin, the Barents Sea has been a site where tensions between Russia and Europe have arisen. Other disputes include one between the United States and Canada in the Beaufort Sea and a 2013 claim to the North Pole by Canada, Russia and, to a lesser extent, Denmark. Differences in interpretation of the Law of the Sea mean future disputes are possible, but even these, in the absence of more general international tension, are resolvable peacefully through existing Arctic institutions.

INTERPRETING THE RULES?

The influence of rules is determined, at least in part, by whether there is a place or a means to settle disputes about what the rules mean. Who judges in the Great North? Do we face an Arctic with law but without courts or other places to seek just decisions? We do not. For one, the Law of the Sea provides a number of ways to resolve legal questions; the spirit is to encourage compliance by recognizing several options to settle disputes—from negotiation to specialized courts. For boundary questions, for example, the Commission on the Limits of the Continental Shelf was created. The commission makes recommendations to states on the establishment of the outer limits of the continental shelf beyond 200 nautical miles.[19] In the Arctic, the five Arctic coastal states already have or soon will hand in their submissions. As of late 2019, the commission was considering submissions made by the Russian Federation for the Arctic Ocean (following up on an earlier submission).[20] The Lomonosov Ridge, a feature that spans a considerable distance across the center of the Arctic Ocean and which has considerable resource value, is addressed in the submission.[21] Based on the argument that this geological formation is a natural extension of their land masses, Russia, Denmark and Canada are each trying to make claims over it. Overlapping claims for continental shelf areas include Canada and Denmark; Canada and the United States; Denmark and Norway; Denmark and Russia; Russia and the United States; and Canada, Denmark and Russia.[22]

But what happens if these disputes are left unresolved is unknown. Or what if, under a specific interpretation of these articles, the commission's decisions are rejected? Rulings may not be binding under customary international law.[23] It is also possible that resource battles could develop in the seabed following the International Seabed Authority's actions. Exploration and exploitation carried out "for the benefit of mankind as a whole" may mean one thing to a country with companies capable of mining for minerals and something else to those poorer nations which favor a distribution of revenue from the riches recovered from the deep sea.

Interpretations of other parts of the treaty with no (or at first nonobvious) links to the environment affect Arctic conditions and may be made in a number of tribunals. An example is the strange connection between the Law of the Sea section on piracy and protection of Arctic resources that arose in the Russian piracy case. The Law of the Sea notes thus:

> Piracy consists of any of the following acts:
>
> (a) any illegal acts of violence or detention, or any act of depredation, committed for private ends by the crew or the passengers of a private ship or a private aircraft, and directed:
> (i) on the high seas, against another ship or aircraft, or against persons or property on board such ship or aircraft;
> (ii) against a ship, aircraft, persons or property in a place outside the jurisdiction of any State. [24]

UNCLOS obliges nations to cooperate in the repression of piracy, and any nation can seize pirate ships and aircraft, arrest persons and seize property on board. In the *Arctic Sunrise* case, Greenpeace protesters on a ship flying the Dutch flag attempted to scale a Russian drilling platform. What they intended to do on it was a matter of disagreement although Greenpeace was engaged in a campaign: "Save the Arctic." The activists said they wished to place some flags to protest drilling but they also said in a tweet: "We're going to try and stop the drilling." The Russians took control of the ship, which was then in Russia's exclusive economic zone, and they arrested—the protesters said with force—people who had attached themselves to the oil platform.

The *Arctic Sunrise* was towed to the Russian port of Murmansk. There all on board were taken to a detention facility. A Russian court issued a warrant to arrest all 30 people, many of whom were kept in custody for weeks. They were first charged with piracy, a crime in Russia with a strict jail sentence; this was later changed to "aggravated hooliganism."

The Netherlands asked for immediate release of the ship and its shipmates to Dutch authorities. The Dutch said that the ship was in open sea—and hence outside Russian jurisdiction. Russia did not release the ship; so the Netherlands filed a case in the International Tribunal for the Law of the Sea. In 2013, the tribunal ordered Moscow to release the *Arctic Sunrise* and its crew, who should be allowed to leave Russia with a bail of 3.5 million Euro. Later, the International Permanent Court of Arbitration, another dispute resolution body, ruled that Russia had breached the Law of the Sea Treaty. The tribunal ruled that the actions of Greenpeace could not be labelled as piracy or hooliganism, and it required that the Dutch be compensated for damages to the ship. For its part, Russia did not, in this case, recognize the authority of the court. But the tribunal's actions were internationally recognized and influential.

BEYOND THE LAW OF THE SEA

There are numerous other sources of environmental rules for the Arctic. The International Maritime Organization (IMO) is a major player in managing activities in the marine environment. It does so through the use of treaties and soft laws. In 2017, the IMO Polar Code entered into force. It bans discharges of ship oil residues in the polar regions. One part covers safety; a second, pollution prevention. It requires that food waste be property managed and encourages ships not to use or carry heavy oil in the Arctic.

A major step in international cooperation in and for the Arctic came into effect in 2021. In 2018, the five Arctic Ocean coastal States (Canada, Denmark [acting on behalf of Greenland and the Faroe Islands], Norway, Russia and the United States) as well as China, the European Union (EU), Iceland, Japan and

South Korea signed the Agreement to Prevent Unregulated High Seas Fisheries in the Central Arctic Ocean (CAOF Agreement or CAOFA). Its objective is to prevent unregulated fishing in the Central Arctic Ocean—the Arctic's largest area of high seas which is as big as the Mediterranean Sea—through the application of precautionary conservation and management measures to ensure sustainable use of fish stocks. CAOFA covers fish, mollusks and crustaceans, but not sedentary species as defined by UNCLOS.[25] The agreement has a sunset clause, which means that it is subject to ending (in 16 years) but it will be automatically renewed unless one of the parties objects.[26] Underscoring the perspective of sustainability embracing cultural traditions, the agreement integrates principles of the United Nations Declaration on the Rights of Indigenous Peoples in international law-making.[27]

The Svalbard Treaty, ratified by dozens of nations, also addresses sharing of fishing rights in parts of the Arctic. The wording of the CAOF agreement was aimed to avoid conclusions on the status of waters around Svalbard (or Spitsbergen) where Norway has fisheries jurisdiction, but where other nations have rights to engage in fishing and other marine activities.

Some rules do not include all states, not even all Arctic states, nor all peoples of the Arctic. Bilateral (two-country agreements) include the 1983 Canada-Denmark Agreement wherein the two nations agreed to cooperate and protect the marine environment within their areas of responsibility. Then there are activities of regional groups such as the Barents Euro-Arctic Council (BEAR), which promotes sustainable economic and social development in the Barents Region.[28] For subnational governments and the Saami Council, the Barents Regional Council (BRC) promotes cooperation and development.[29] In both Barents organizations, indigenous peoples have advisory roles.[30]

In addition, many domestic laws have Arctic reach. These include, as introduced in Chapter 2, the 1971 Alaska Native Claims Settlement Act, the 1975 James Bay and Northern Quebec Treaty and the 1984 Inuvialuit land claims agreement. Also influential are the 1979 Greenland Home Rule Accord, the Yukon land claims treaties and aboriginal self-government agreements of 1992, the Finnmark Act, the Greenland Self-Government Agreement and the Saami Convention. The Constitution Act of Canada provides for indigenous rights and requirements of consulting with indigenous peoples.[31] Certain rules address the important point of who is at the table in making rules about Arctic sustainability. Some experts consider these rules more important than more well-publicized treaties and predict they will have great influence in managing the Arctic in the twenty-first century. As one Arctic observer put it in the UCI

Arctic Expert Survey: for some reason, few in Copenhagen, Helsinki, Moscow, Ottawa, Stockholm and Washington yet seem to understand the enormous impacts of Arctic devolution, co-management agreements and land claims settlements.[32]

RULES FOR PARTICULAR ARCTIC PROBLEMS

Hole in the sky?

The Arctic has a central place in the story of the famous ozone hole introduced in Chapter 3. Starting with a treaty named the Montreal Protocol, a number of rules have aimed to control and eventually ban worldwide the production and use of chemicals that weaken the ozone layer, a protective section of the earth's atmosphere within the stratosphere. The substances, now in the aggregate called ozone depleting substances, were ubiquitous after World War II when they came to be used in air conditioners, spray cans, refrigerators and many other consumer products. They were considered benign with no toxic effects until the chemical reaction which lead to creation of the ozone hole was discovered. Rapidly for a world response, a system of legal controls on these chemicals, beginning with chlorofluorocarbons (CFCs), was adopted. In 1976, an initiative began with United Nations actions—at first modest because the full effects of the chemical reaction and its effects on humans (cataracts, skin cancers and the like) and nature (destruction of phytoplankton, for example) were not fully appreciated. Quickly, however, science established that these effects were becoming increasingly alarming, and the nations of the world developed an elegant treaty group.

The Montreal system does not target only the Arctic itself, but, as with the Antarctic, it is a direct beneficiary of the rules—the first to address fully the global nature of a set of pollutants. Without international cooperation, efforts to cut back on production in one country would likely be offset by activities elsewhere. A classic free-rider problem would exist: I benefit from continuing to pollute and benefit because my competitors have stopped polluting with products we both can make.

In the Arctic, as with other parts of the world including the more famous Antarctica "hole," the new rules mean that the ozone layer should be repaired in a few decades—the hole "closed," metaphorically. There will be years when the Arctic ozone layer oscillates, and global climate change will counter some of the positive results. Ozone depleting substances account for about half of the global warming in the Arctic, making their control important for more than the need to repair the ozone layer.

Threatened Creatures

A complex web of national and international rules exists to protect endangered or threatened species, some iconic or lovable (at least from a distance) in the Arctic, as for the world. Globally, a main treaty is the Convention on the International Trade in Endangered Species of Flora and Fauna, generally called CITES. CITES controls the trade in selected plants and animals protecting them through regulation of import, export and reexport (and introduction from the sea). The nature of the requirements depends on how serious is the challenge to extinction that a species confronts; different levels of vulnerability are published in appendices to the treaty.[33] Among the species found in the Arctic with varying degrees of protection are whales (the fin, the bowhead, the sperm, the humpbacked, the Minke, the killer and the Beluga), the white-tailed eagle, the polar bear and the walrus. Arctic species of particular popularity that are not affected are seal, reindeer and musk oxen.

Protecting endangered species is often a source of conflict among environmentalists and others (over critters ranging from owls to snail darters and salmon). One person's sentient endangered animal is another person's meal, source of a rite of passage—or a dangerous predator or a job destroyer. So rules on species protection make their way to international courts for interpretation. One particularly hard-fought case in the Arctic involves seals, including the sweet looking big-eyed seal pup. Rules under the World Trade Organization (WTO) law were at issue.

For decades, many observers have expressed outrage over the Arctic seal hunts. In season, thousands of pups are shot and then clubbed to death. Luxury goods are made with the seal skins and furs. These commercial sealing operations, proponents of anti-hunting rules have argued, are inherently cruel and inhumane. Like many environmental fights, celebrities have assumed front-page parts in the anti-hunting campaigns. Paul McCartney, Brigitte Bardot and Pamela Anderson have spoken out against the hunt. Anderson, along with one of the creators of *The Simpsons*, offered a novelty check for $1 million to the Canadian Sealers Association to end the practice. Anthony Bourdain, however, suggesting the range of opinions that feed into environmental rule making, wrote "I'm all for protecting seals, but a total ban dooms the indigenous people above [the] Arctic Circle to death or relocation […] I completely understand well-meaning intentions of good hearted chefs who signed this petition. But they are wrong. Visit the Inuit."[34] Supporters of the annual seal hunts say they provide important income for fishery workers and that the hunts are valuable parts of traditional cultural practices.

Rules aimed to stop the hunts have been adopted in many places. Among the most important were in the EU. Its Seal Regime bans the sale of seal products in all EU states, with a few exceptions including for products from hunts by indigenous peoples. The ban specifically targets commercial sealing operations, such as those in two Arctic nations, Canada and Norway. The two nations complained in a case brought before the WTO. A "lower court" or panel of the WTO found that the EU's ban on imported seal products is justified under a section of trade rules involving protection of public morals, here specifically on the grounds of animal welfare. But the ban was discriminatory in the way applied; it needed to be changed to comply with global trade rules. The EU had not made comparable efforts to facilitate access of the Canadian Inuit to the exception to the hunting ban as it did for the Greenlandic Inuit. WTO rejected an appeal by Canada and Norway, setting a precedent that animal welfare can prevail over the right to trade.

The dispute was one of the most polarizing and complex in WTO history, and marked the first time that the WTO body accepted animal welfare as moral grounds for justifying a country's violation of the global trade body's "most favored nation" principle[35] which requires equal treatment of all countries in a trade group. Both sides claimed victory. Canadian Ministers said that "the ban on seal products adopted in the European Union was a political decision that has no basis in fact or science [...]. We are pleased that today's decision [...] confirms what we have said all along, namely that the EU's seal regime is arbitrarily and unjustifiably applied."[36] Norwegian officials were also pleased with the ruling, saying that it established "that the EU cannot impose arbitrary measures in this way."[37] Brussels too described a victory: the EU was within its rights to ban seal products on moral grounds.

Canadian Inuit, reflecting on the general indigenous concern over "protective" rulemaking, were not pleased. The exception they said was designed without the input of indigenous peoples. They labeled the public morals argument as "abhorrent." Inuit Leader Terry Audla said, "It is morally reprehensible for anyone to impede those goals—which are the basic rights of any citizens of the world [...] Inuit live according to the principles of fairness and compassion and we seek nothing more than to feed our families and make an honest living in the modern economy." This was another failure to consult with indigenous people.

Later, the governments of Nunavut, the Northwest Territories and Greenland reported that the exemption and its certification process to allow products into European markets had failed to assist with socioeconomic development. They requested that the EU help raise public awareness of the exemption for

Inuit communities, including allowing the Inuit/Inuvialuit to advocate among European consumers. Greenland reiterated that "the trade in seal products is a legitimate and sustainable activity that should not be hampered or stigmatized, and that animal welfare is a concern to Inuit or other Indigenous communities."[38] Denmark was the only EU member state reported to having imported seal products under the indigenous exception.

Even more law ...

Many other legal commitments have been made in addition to the major treaties and rules laid out in Table 4.1. Some rules are more localized but important. In 1994, the United States and the Russian Federation entered an Agreement on Cooperation in the Prevention of Pollution of the Environment in the Arctic. Seal conservation was the subject of an agreement between the Government of Canada and the Government of Norway in 1971. Other rules cover caribou and bird protection, oil pollution and air-born pollution—to name a few.[39]

Decades ago, the United Nations Environment Programme (UNEP) created something called the Regional Seas Programme. In order to protect the great seas and oceans of the world, countries were to work together to develop and implement "comprehensive action plans" for the protection and development of some of the world's seas. Some programs adopt treaties on specific great seas problems, like pollution run-off from land, erosion of the coasts, dying fish species. There are now 13 regional seas programs; about half are administered by the UNEP. They cover the world from the Black Sea to the South-East Pacific. Strategies that regional seas entities have adopted include several relevant to the Arctic. They create guidelines for the control of marine pollution and for the protection of aquatic resources and to study effects on human health and ecosystems. The Arctic program is a "partner program;" partner means that the connection of the sea or region to the United Nations is less formal than for other seas, such as for the Mediterranean—one of the oldest and most active programs. There are calls for formalizing and strengthening the program in the Arctic to move in the direction of making rules.[40]

The Arctic Council—influencing rules

Initiatives that influence the quality of the Arctic's social and physical environment do not only include specific rules. An organization that is playing a central place in the Arctic world and beyond is the Arctic Council. The council is a forum that promotes cooperation, coordination and interaction among the

Arctic nations and the Arctic peoples (indigenous and others). The story of its birth and growth is a surprising one.

Among the notable reforms that Soviet Secretary Mikhail Gorbachev made in opening the Soviet Union to the world was to propose that the Arctic states cooperate in various fields. The set of interactions which Gorbachev set in place led to the creation of the Arctic Council. The Soviet initiative was motivated in large part by concerns over the effects of the Soviet Union's dumping, over a period of years, of radioactive and other hazardous materials into the Arctic Ocean. Secretary Gorbachev was willing to confront these problems. In 1987, he said:[41]

> A new, democratic philosophy of international relations, of world politics is breaking through […] Our policy is an invitation to dialogue, to a search, to a better world, to normalization of international relations […] The substantive and frank East-West dialogue, far from proving fruitless for both sides, has become a distinguishing feature of contemporary world politics […] Comrades, speaking in Murmansk the capital of the Soviet Polar Region [where he was], it is appropriate to examine the idea of cooperation between all people also from the standpoint of the situation in the northern part of this planet […] The Arctic is not only the Arctic Ocean, but also the northern tips of three continents: Europe, Asia and America. It is the place where the Eurasian, North American and Asian Pacific regions meet, where the frontiers come close to one another and the interests of states belonging to mutually opposed military blocs and nonaligned ones cross […] Therefore, while in Murmansk, and standing on the threshold of the Arctic and the North Atlantic, I would like to invite, first of all, the countries of the region to a discussion on the burning security issues.
>
> How do we visualize this? It is possible to take simultaneously the roads of bilateral and multilateral cooperation. I have had the opportunity to speak on the subject of "our common European home" on more than one occasion. The potential of contemporary civilization could permit us to make the Arctic habitable for the benefit of the national economies and other human interests of the near-Arctic states, for Europe and the entire international community […] Let the North of the globe, the Arctic, become a zone of peace. Let the North Pole be a pole of peace […] Through joint efforts it could be possible to work out an overall concept of rational development of northern areas […] the scientific exploration of the Arctic is of immense importance for the whole of mankind. We have a wealth of experience here and are prepared to share it. In turn, we are interested in the studies

> conducted in other sub-Arctic and northern countries [...] We propose [...] a conference of sub-Arctic states on coordinating research in the Arctic. The conference could consider the possibility of setting up a joint Arctic Research Council. Should the partners agree, Murmansk could host the conference [...] Questions bearing on the interests of the indigenous population of the North, the study of its ethnic distinctions and the development of cultural ties between northern peoples require special attention. The urgency of this is obvious.
>
> The Soviet Union proposes drawing up jointly an integrated comprehensive plan for protecting the natural environment of the North. The North European countries could set an example to others by reaching an agreement on establishing a system to monitor the state of the natural environment and radiation safety in the region. We must hurry to protect the nature of the tundra, forest tundra and the northern forest areas.
>
> We are ready to discuss any counter proposals and ideas. The main thing is to conduct affairs so that the climate here is determined by the warm Gulfstream of the European process and not by the Polar chill of accumulated suspicions and prejudices [...] What everybody can be absolutely certain of is the Soviet Union's profound and certain interest in preventing the North of the planet, its Polar and sub-Polar regions and all Northern countries from ever again becoming an arena of war, and in forming there a genuine zone of peace and fruitful cooperation.

These prophetic words, this invitation to work together, led to what is today the Arctic Council.

Now, if you visit Tromsø, one of the most northern cities in the world, you will walk past a stately wooden church, an adult shop, several welcoming restaurants and bars with warming candles flickering outside, and then arrive at the Fram Center, the home of the Arctic Council. It is in a tall office building overlooking Polari, an Arctic aquarium educational center. On an upper floor of the Fram Center are the sparkling glass and light wood rooms of the Secretariat of the Arctic Council. The council evolved from the events that followed on soon after Secretary Gorbachev's speech.

In 1991, Finland convened a conference of the eight Arctic states in Rovaniemi. There they signed the Rovaniemi Declaration, adopting the Arctic Environmental Protection Strategy, a nonbinding agreement among the Arctic nations. In a rare outcome for international institutions, some indigenous peoples of the Arctic were also represented through the Indigenous Peoples

Secretariat. It is composed of three Permanent Participants: the Saami Council (Nordic and Western Russia); the Inuit Circumpolar Conference (United States, Canada, Greenland and Russia); and the Association of Indigenous Minorities of the North, Siberia and the Far East of the Russian Federation. This relationship was soon formalized. In 1996, the eight Arctic nations signed a declaration that created the Arctic Council. Its mandate is fairly broad, but it does not address military security. Now the Arctic Athabaskan, Aleut, Gwich'in, Inuit, Sámi, and the 41 indigenous peoples of the Russian Association of Indigenous Peoples of the North, as Permanent Participants, sit at the council meetings along with elected and appointed government officials.

The eight countries with territory in the region have full membership, including voting rights in the council. Observers are China, France, Germany, India, Italy, Japan, the Netherlands, Poland, Singapore, South Korea, Spain and the UK. At first look, the make-up seems almost random, but these countries and many others see a warmer, more accessible, and resource-rich region with potential national benefits; they want to enter the existing Arctic institutions and learn how to work within them—or perhaps around or against them.

The council has evolved from a fairly obscure international organization that made few contributions to rules to being one of considerable importance to the Arctic environment. The council normally creates nonbinding guidelines, but it has also had a role in creating some treaties. The first binding treaty that the council promoted, on search and rescue, recognized the increased use of Arctic waters for tourism, shipping, research and resource development. Two other agreements, one on cooperation on oil and the other on scientific cooperation, were later entered. There are valuable side outcomes of the council's work. Meetings of the council bring together world leaders who often explore matters of Arctic sustainability cooperation (and occasionally) conflict in informal candid ways. And the council's work groups offer sustained opportunities for sharing of scientific and policy expertise across nations and environmental organizations.

SOFT LAW: RULES?

Countries also often act in accordance with Soft Law. Over the years of modern international law in meetings and conferences, such as in Stockholm in the early 1970s and in Rio in 1992, delegates from all over the world have articulated concepts they wish to be influential: aspirations for the protection of the planet. This unfamiliar term, soft law, refers to principles that may later structure more formal rules and, in the meantime, can guide discussion, negotiations and even decisions. An example is the Precautionary Principle. Found in the preambles of some treaties and widely referred to by negotiators and scholars, it states, to use the form coming from the 1992 Rio environmental meeting, thus:

> Where there are threats of serious or irreversible damage, lack of full scientific certainty shall not be used as a reason for postponing cost-effective measures to prevent environmental degradation.[42]

A statement like this communicates a general sentiment toward environmental protection. Also, it leaves wide discretion for countries to indicate they are following it. Soft law has its weaknesses, as this example makes clear. What is full scientific certainty? It exists nowhere or almost nowhere in science. The concept of cost effectiveness is also immensely plastic and provides room for officials to choose different time periods, and many or few effects. What is serious damage to the environment? Nonetheless, soft law is used in many arguments for actions, or challenges to actions, globally. The Precautionary Principle is often mentioned in concerns for Arctic sustainability. It, in fact, served as an underlying force for the CAOFA, described earlier, creating an agreement regarding fishing before widespread fishing was even feasible in the Arctic.

Also within the inventory of "soft," in 2015 the United Nations stated a set of international goals for sustainable development. There are 17 goals for sustainable development; here are a few that are most relevant to the Arctic:

- Goal 4. Ensure inclusive and equitable quality education and promote lifelong learning opportunities for all
- Goal 5. Achieve gender equality and empower all women and girls
- Goal 6. Ensure availability and sustainable management of water and sanitation for all
- Goal 7. Ensure access to affordable, reliable, sustainable and modern energy for all
- Goal 8. Promote sustained, inclusive and sustainable economic growth, full and productive employment and decent work for all
- Goal 9. Build resilient infrastructure, promote inclusive and sustainable industrialization and foster innovation
- Goal 13. Take urgent action to combat climate change and its impacts [...]
- Goal 14. Conserve and sustainably use the oceans, seas and marine resources for sustainable development[43]

The scope of the goals suggests one of the weaknesses of some forms of soft law—that is, it may complicate the interpretations of other hard law rules.

No doubt amenable to rhetorical response, manipulation and public relations offensives, the goals are nonetheless often cited as checklists for evaluating proposed actions with possible global environmental effects. And a level of benchmarks, although general, is provided following the goals in an attempt to make them more objective. For example, for Goal 6, applicable widely and relevant to the Arctic: "By 2030, improve water quality by reducing pollution, eliminating dumping and minimizing release of hazardous chemicals and materials, halving the proportion of untreated wastewater and substantially increasing recycling and safe reuse globally."

DECLARE NO MORE BIG RULES?

In 2008, the five Arctic coastal states (Canada, Denmark, Norway, the Russian Federation and the United States) adopted the Ilulissat Declaration. It concluded that there is no need for a new comprehensive international legal regime to govern the Arctic ocean.[44] This strong statement of coastal state authority is a potential challenge to the other members of the Arctic Council—and to the rest of the world:

> By virtue of their sovereignty, sovereign rights and jurisdiction in large areas of the Arctic Ocean the five coastal states are in a unique position to address these possibilities and challenges [...] we recall that an extensive international legal framework applies to the Arctic Ocean [...] Notably, the law of the sea provides for important rights and obligations concerning the delineation of the outer limits of the continental shelf, the protection of the marine environment, including ice-covered areas, freedom of navigation, marine scientific research, and other uses of the sea. We remain committed to this legal framework and to the orderly settlement of any possible overlapping claims.[45]

National Law

Rules for Arctic environmental protection and sustainability also come from the environmental laws of the individual Arctic states themselves—that is, laws that apply in their Arctic territories. The inventory here is large. Many of the Arctic countries require environmental impact assessment (consider the environmental consequences before making a decision on actions that may harm the environment). Arctic countries have laws on coastal zone management, endangered species law, fisheries protection law and wetland protection, to name but a few.

Also laws that are not labeled as environmental often have great influence on the environment: tax code requirements, securities filings obligations, general prohibitions against fraud and misuse of the mails and so on. National rules can also extend in reach outside of a country; this exercise of power is called the extraterritorial reach of domestic law. Countries may claim extraterritorial effects for various reasons: one is a state's national security interest. There are several sources of this authority; Principle 21 of the Stockholm Declaration is one.[46]

Indigenous law

Agreements between indigenous peoples and a federal or other government in a country also apply to Arctic protection. So too do rules for interactions between indigenous peoples and private sector businesses and other entities. Accords with indigenous peoples are increasingly respected, especially under federal and national reforms recognizing their claims such as the Nunavut Land Claims Agreement (Nunavut Agreement) and the Alaskan land claims acts described in Chapter 2. Other more specific rules include the Nunavut Fishery Regulations which aim to ensure fish stocks sustainably and which recognize the Inuit's existing approach to fisheries management and harvesting rights—a matter central to sustainability of traditions and culture.[47]

RULES FROM THE COURTS

The Sea Shepherd, the seal pups and the *Arctic Sunrise* Russian piracy cases are part of the law of the Arctic. Climate change law, in fits and starts, also develops in the courts.[48] A flurry of court challenges centers here, and some are Arctic based. Cases have brought considerable attention to the conditions and, in cases, the plight of Arctic indigenous peoples and the values they hold. The actions have various names depending on where they are brought. People can litigate in national courts, file petitions in international tribunals or institutions and make submissions to specialized international institutions.

National court cases

About 400 people live in Kivalina, an Inupiat Eskimo village on a long Alaskan barrier island of about four square miles (10.78 square kilometers). Climate change is affecting the village dramatically. Global warming has altered the thickness, extent and duration of sea ice along the village's coast—now battered by erosion, waves and storm surges. Property damage is extensive, and the village will cease to be unless it relocates. The US Government Accountability Office concluded that the right combination of storm events could flood the entire village at any time. To stay on site is not a viable option for the community. Moving the village will cost about $100 million.[49] The village sued over two dozen energy companies in a California court. It charged that the companies' massive greenhouse gas emissions resulted in global warming, leading to severe erosion of the land where the city is located. The suit, brought under the garden-variety law of nuisance, argued that the companies knew that their operations were causing harm and conspired to keep it secret. The lawsuit failed; the court concluded that this is a politically charged conflict that the courts are unfit to resolve. But Kivalina is one example of the use of a strategy that started with some innovative lawyers in a small number of cases. Quickly it grew in size. The number of cases jumped to 106 in 2016. All told, there have been over 1,400 climate change related claims brought before US courts.[50] The number will grow as the ravages of climate change do, and as science more accurately indicates specific causes and exposes those responsible for the damages. In 2013, scientists linked 63 percent of cumulative worldwide greenhouse gas emissions from 1854 to 2010 to just 90 companies. In 2015, the International Energy Agency used data to estimate the total amount of emissions from the top 20 greenhouse gas-emitting countries. The United States came in second, behind China.

Several cases have specifically targeted the Arctic or ultimately affect the Arctic. In 2013, environmental groups unsuccessfully challenged the US Environmental Protection Agency's permits that authorized exploratory drilling in the Arctic Ocean. The permits will result in Shell emitting more than 250 tons of pollutants every year. Environmentalists argued that greenhouse gases and black carbon from ships would accelerate the melting of the snow pack and sea ice in the Arctic in native Alaskan communities.[51] That corporations are at least partially responsible for melting glaciers has been argued in a non-Arctic case but one that may influence law beyond Germany where it was brought. A Peruvian farmer sued RWE, Germany's largest electricity provider.[52] He claims that RWE knew at least to some extent that its emissions of greenhouse gases contributed to global warming and that the company should therefore be liable for damages. In a creative argument, the farmer recognized that RWE is only one contributor to global warming; he asked that RWE pay for its estimated annual contribution to global warming. Claims under another US law, the Endangered Species Act, involve the listing (or more precisely the failure to list) and the conservation of threatened and endangered species.[53] Most US courts have held that the effects of climate change need to be considered when deciding whether to list species and determining their habitats, including in the Arctic. In one case, pinpointing a habitat for polar bears was allowed to go forward even though the area was an industrial staging area for oil and gas operations.[54]

There are many more law suits: an environmental law group sues a natural gas provider for negligent management of pipelines; governments are sued for alleged illegal approval of oil and gas projects; governments themselves claim public nuisance for the way energy companies run their power plants. Some cases focus on procedures: a hamlet sues for failure to consult with indigenous peoples on seismic testing in the Arctic.[55] Cases charge that company officials knew, or should have known, about the climate impacts of their activities.

International courts

The Circumpolar Conference, a nongovernmental indigenous peoples organization, brought a case before an inter-American forum, the Inter-American Commission on Human Rights, an organ of the Organization of American States. It argued that climate change linked to emissions of greenhouse gases in the United States violated their rights to maintain a traditional way of life. In sections which highlight the special importance of climate change in the Arctic, the petition stated thus:

> Several principles of international law guide the application of the human rights issues in this case. Most directly, the United States is obligated by its membership in the Organization of American States and its acceptance of the American Declaration of the Rights and Duties of Man to protect the rights of the Inuit [...] The United States also has international environmental law obligations that are relevant to this petition. For instance, the United States also has an obligation to ensure that activities within its territory do not cause transboundary harm or violate other treaties to which it is a party [...] The impacts of climate change, caused by acts and omissions by the United States, violate the Inuit's fundamental human rights [...] These include their rights to the benefits of culture, to property, to the preservation of health, life, physical integrity, security, and a means of subsistence, and to residence, movement, and inviolability of the home [...] The United States of America, currently the largest contributor to greenhouse emissions in the world, has nevertheless repeatedly declined to take steps to regulate and reduce its emissions of the gases responsible for climate change.[56]

Another case was brought before the Inter-American Commission based on violations of human rights on behalf of the Arctic Athabaskan. The Athabaskan Peoples, who have lived in the Arctic regions of Canada and the United States for 10,000 years, depend on the Arctic climate for survival. They argue that global warming has changed the Arctic climate drastically, damaging their lives, livelihoods and culture. They sought a declaration that Canada's black carbon emissions violate the American Declaration.[57] They also requested an established plan to help mitigate the effects of emissions in the Arctic.

The slow pace of climate progress prompts activists to see these actions as critical and necessary—if not already too late. Nongovernmental organizations and others use litigation where they have been unsuccessful working in the usual political or bureaucratic arena. They see the court system as more impartial and effective than government agencies or majority political parties.

The goals of lawsuits vary: some aim to move to zero emissions, some actions wish to keep all coal in the ground, some seek sustainable development, some emphasize preservation and some push for remediating the damage already caused or paying for it. At times, this range of goals makes it hard to predict who will be the parties on each side. Arctic indigenous peoples across and within tribes or groups do not always agree about what to do with resources in or near their lands and waters. For their parts, some environmentalists consider preservation of the physical environment their raison d'etre—whether taking a comprehensive perspective or having a single focus on the air, water, wildlife (even a specific species) or plastics. Others, however, see the need for some economic development of the Arctic to improve the lives of native people or, perhaps more cynically, because it is important strategically to have the indigenous on their side in litigation. Some environmental advocates want to push government agencies to better enforce the law. Some want money damages. Some simply want to bring attention to climate change's ravages.

A public trust?

A particularly innovative, some say radical, legal argument about climate change uses a centuries old doctrine known as the public trust. The idea is that the atmosphere is, like the seas, a resource which is common to all people. Governments cannot give, sell or more generally convey public trust resources to private entities except in the most constrained circumstances. Common property resources—air, wildlife, water—are held by governments in an endowment. The government is the trustee and it must manage the corpus or resource for present and future generations; the trustees must protect the assets. As put in an early classic case, "the State can no more abdicate its trust over property in which the whole people are interested [...] than it can abdicate its police powers."[58] Based on this doctrine, a movement has arisen. Followers argue that the government has a duty to curtail private appropriation (a type of ownership) of the atmosphere and its use as a dumping ground for carbon pollution and greenhouse gases.[59]

The advocates speak in dramatic, even fateful terms. The earth is entering a period of absolute chaos. An exit strategy out of climate disruption must be implemented immediately. The argument proceeds that there is a scientific prescription that can save the planet. If the prescription is filled and taken, just as with effective medicines for other problems, the planet can get well. This compliance needs the push of lawsuits: those aimed at "decarbonizing the atmosphere" and "drawing down" excess carbon dioxide in it. For the first goal, only a handful of years remains to cut carbon dioxide in the atmosphere to about 350 parts per million. This means the world must make yearly reductions in emissions of a noted percentage, one which gets larger every year that there is no progress. For the second, what is needed is a drawdown, a pull back; the world cannot exceed a given number of gigatons of emissions. This can be achieved through doable activities such as sequestration of CO_2, regenerative grazing and the restoration of wetlands.

At first, many environmental groups, even those which have used the public trust doctrine in their own practices, thought the idea was far-fetched and would fail. But they know that success could require government to create enforceable emission reduction plans and structure injunctions, that is judicial orders to institutions that control activities responsible for climate change. When those bringing them include children, these lawsuits become more compelling.[60] They plead that they and future generations will suffer the greatest injuries of climate change from the government's failure to protect the common atmosphere today.

The public trust doctrine has been applied in national courts in the United States, India,[61] the Netherlands,[62] Pakistan[63]and Uganda.[64] Some mention the Arctic explicitly; others, were they to succeed, would protect the regional environment by limiting fossil fuel exploitation, helping villages hurt by climate change and requiring the study of damage to the Arctic for proposed new projects.

There are, no doubt, big legal barriers to success. The first few cases were dismissed rather readily. But several cases have achieved significant advances in the courts. In 2016, an Oregon court ruled that minors had standing, that is they are appropriate people to bring a lawsuit, to make the public trust claim.

An appeals court, in 2018, ruled in favor of the children, denying the Trump administration's attempt to squash the suit.[65] But later on appeal the court ruled that the children lacked standing to pursue their claims.[66]

In the Arctic, erosion, extreme weather events, scorching high temperatures, loss of hunting and fishing habitat as well as destruction of traditional villages will continue for some time regardless of the success of activities that aim to cut greenhouse gases. Communities from Kivalina to Iqaluit face expenses, great costs of response and repair—what climate change experts call adaptation. So some cases attempt to address this side of the climate change challenge seeking, for example, to require management plans for energy facilities that threaten the nearby environment.[67] Others build on indigenous peoples' rights to lands and resources traditionally occupied or used by them; for example the Indigenous and Tribal Peoples Convention provides arguments to pursue climate legal actions in the Arctic.[68]

Effectiveness / Enough?

Does this encyclopedia of rules come together to adequately protect the North? Do we need more rules to have a sustainable Arctic? In responding to these questions for the Arctic, law should be understood in the larger context of society, as a tool that can be used, abused and manipulated by those who are influential in society more generally.

These rules taken in the context of forces that work to preserve the environment and culture suggest a positive future of Arctic sustainability. Law and other influencers are used strategically in social movements and in what has come to be known as civil society, the nonofficial groups, nongovernmental organizations, charities, service organizations, churches and associations with clear social goals that are important to how societies make and implement law, educate and distribute resources.

For the Arctic, civil society is strong and becoming more influential every year. It includes hundreds of groups committed to the region: nongovernmental groups like the Association of World Reindeer Herders; environmental groups, such as the World Wide Fund for Nature; churches; unions; scientific organizations, such as the International Arctic Social Sciences Association; and elected officials meeting in other roles such as the Standing Committee of the Parliamentarians of the Arctic Region. We have seen how indigenous groups have come to have considerable influence: the Saami Council, the Inuit Circumpolar Council, the Arctic Athabaskan Council, the Aleutian International Association and the Gwich'in Council International. Whether these should be understood as another part of civil society or as official entities is a separate question. These activists work to constrain what official leadership can do.[69] They also influence what that leadership knows about the conditions of and needs in the Arctic. They assist in how questions and answers may be framed. They share knowledge of all kinds. They align with governments seeking particular outcomes, language in law, outcomes in conflicts and enforcement of rules. An example is how indigenous peoples were central in arguing that the ban on seal pup skins negatively affects the market for all seal products. Inuit groups supported Canada and Norway when those countries challenged the EU Regulation as chronicled earlier.[70] This part of civil society led to the EU passing a resolution recognizing

> "the wish of the inhabitants and governments of the Arctic region with sovereign rights and responsibilities to continue to pursue sustainable economic development while at the same time protecting the traditional sources of the Indigenous peoples' livelihoods and the very sensitive nature of the Arctic ecosystems.[71]

With or without active civil society, opinions vary about the quality and adequacy of the rules. People on the street, academics, politicians and policymakers disagree within their own groups and across them. The World Wildlife Foundation grades Arctic nations on topics important to the Arctic environment. Canada earned the most As—three for its successes in ecosystems-based management, control of black carbon and methane pollution, and effective management of oil spills. The United States and Denmark got the most Ds; they both received a D for shipping control, and the United States got a D for ineffective biodiversity protection and Denmark had this same grade for insufficient protection of its conservation areas. Overall, across the countries graded, good marks were given for ecosystems-based management and use of environmental impact and risk assessment and poor marks for recognition of the equal partner status of indigenous peoples in Arctic management.[72]

Legal rules that are most often characterized as helpful include in the marine environment: UNCLOS, the Polar Code, regional efforts to create Marine Protected Areas, and specific fishing stocks protection. For the air environment, good grades are often given for the Persistent Organic Pollution Convention, the Paris Agreement, the Ozone regime, controls on black carbon and, although very recent, the Minamata Convention on Mercury. As for species protection, whaling, seal, and walrus management; the Polar Bear Treaty; and rules on biodiversity protection have been at least somewhat successful. For required procedures, Arctic observers find valuable requirements of consultation with indigenous peoples, cooperation across governments and environmental impact assessments.

Yet for some, there is great skepticism about whether law even matters. In our survey of Arctic experts, a small but vociferous minority thought the focus on new law was misplaced:[73]

> None of these things [an RSP (Regional Seas Programme), new treaties, expansion of Arctic Council] will make much of a difference, at all, to what's happening in the Arctic natural environment [...] [I]t's just lawyers and affiliates wasting time and effort on weak and ineffectual documents that are never enforced.

And:

> I don't think international environmental law is needed or will help improving things. It will just add a layer of bureaucracy,

And:

> More LAW doesn't guarantee better protection, sometimes the contrary as instruments can be seen as not convenient for States to be bound by them.

More:

> Drafting national laws on the Arctic environment without the full consultation with Arctic residents, indigenous and settler, is a complete waste of time and money. The people in the air-conditioned cubicles in the national capitals know little and understand less about northern realities.

And:

> Focus should be on fewer, and more important matters, rather than attempting to regulate as much as possible, and regulating for the sake of regulating. A typical example of unnecessary over-regulation is the EU Seal Regime.

The World Ocean Assessment described the influence of all the rules in a refreshingly jargon-free way: "tasks are split among many players: unless each knows how the part they play fits into the overall pattern, there are risks of confusion, contradictory actions and failure to act."[74]

Conclusions about effectiveness need to be put into the larger question of *Polar Shift*. Legal rules, of all kinds, are not alone in the goal to protect and sustain the Arctic. Do rules *with other* influencers—science and education, social movements, philanthropy, research, civic action—add up to enough to achieve an acceptable future of the Arctic environment? We have seen that many experts focus on protecting the Arctic environment through other institutions, independently or working through the law. These initiatives either supplement the influence of rules or carry on indifferent to the rules. Philanthropy and education are among them.

Many foundations support Arctic sustainability. Some, like the Alaska Conservation Foundation, work in individual states, provinces or territories. Others focus on individual Arctic needs; for example, the Global Greengrants Fund makes grants to Arctic coastal communities. A village that was funded had voted to relocate to escape rising sea levels and the impacts of climate change. The fund calls this a locally relevant solution.[75] The wide range of the goals of the giving foundations mirrors views about what it means to protect and sustain the Arctic. The Nordic Environment Finance Corporation, a financial institution established in 1990 by a treaty among Denmark, Finland, Iceland, Norway and Sweden, aims "to generate positive environmental impact of interest to the Nordic countries [...] by facilitating investments related to green growth and climate mitigation and adaptation globally.[76] Guggenheim's Arctic Investment Protocol, started in 2016 and evolved a year later through the Economic Forum into the Arctic Economic Council (AEC), is a business forum dedicated to responsible economic development in the Arctic. Its work is as an example of a movement broadly labeled as corporate social responsibility. While criticized by some main environmental organizations for promoting development that damages the physical environment, the initiative presents itself as promoting sustainability. (Its understandings of that term is not shared by some environmental activists when making decisions on specific projects.)[77] There are several other sources of funds geared toward the Arctic environment. Table 4.2 lists just some of the funders.

Many of these sources are modest, but taken together this philanthropy is significant. Even where amounts are small, target grants can make a difference to individual aspects of environmental damage in the Arctic. Yet available monies, public or private, will never be enough. Estimates of the costs to the world's economies just to slow down emissions run into the multiple billions.

Education [...] Many small changes can make a big change.

Table 4.2 Foundations and Funds for Arctic Environmental Activities

Alaska Conservation Foundation serves as funder and supportive resource for a community of nonprofits working to protect and wisely manage Alaska's natural resources. (https://alaskaconservation.org/about/mission/)
Global Greengrants Fund makes grants in the Arctic to address climate change, protect traditional ways of life and preserve natural resources. (https://www.greengrants.org/where-we-work/north-america/)
Guggenheim Partners endorses World Economic Forum's Arctic Investment Protocol. (https://www.guggenheimpartners.com/firm/news/guggenheim-partners-endorses-world-economic-forums) (https://www.theguardian.com/environment/2011/nov/16/guggenheim-partners-arctic-investment-fund)
Nordic Environment Finance Corporation facilitates investments related to green growth and climate migration and adaptation globally, with particular focus on Eastern Europe, the Baltic Sea, the Arctic and Barents regions. (https://www.nefco.org/about-nefco/)
Office of Polar Programs supports Arctic and Antarctic science through grants to researchers across the United States and by providing polar facilities and operational support. (https://www.nsf.gov/div/index.jsp?div=OPP)
Russian State Hydrometeorological University provides education, training and research in meteorology, hydrometeorology, oceanology, climate change and related environmental and social disciplines. (https://education.uarctic.org/universities/russia/8400/russian-state-hydrometeorological-university)
Center for Arctic and Climate Research focuses on research and education programs and projects in the Russian Arctic regions (https://www.pmel.noaa.gov/arctic-zone/orgs.html).
Bellona Foundation in Norway identifies and implements sustainable solutions to environmental problems: climate change, the environmental impact of the oil and gas industry in Europe and Russia as well as the cleanup after the legacy of the Cold War in Russia. (https://bellona.org/)
The Arctic Slope Community Foundation Fund addresses the needs of people living within the Arctic Slope Region. (https://alaskacf.org/blog/funds/arctic-slope-community-foundation-fund/)
World Arctic Fund supports researchers with special interests in the Arctic region. (https://www.worldarcticfund.org/)

A second essential influence is education, which is central to the protection of the Arctic environment. One common refrain among those who want immediate Arctic protection is "Who can be opposed to education's enhancement?"—it is a motherhood and apple pie question. It is facile to conclude it is needed. It is however not enough. That position may be accurate, but before improvements are made in law and society, people must gain a better understanding of the science of sustainability in the Arctic, how the behaviors of people as well as industries and governments determine good and bad futures for the Arctic, how to link indigenous or traditional knowledge with other forms of knowing, the impacts of development in the region, how environmental law works and how it can be made to work better.

The call for environmental education has been part of the environmental movement since its beginnings. Despite conclusions that "we don't have time for more study" or that further education "puts off action now," education is a crucial support for other initiatives to protect the North. If people understand environmental changes, their dynamics and proposed solutions, they will be more accepting of new rules, more willing to give in one form or another to Arctic protection.

In our survey of Arctic experts, the most common choice of approaches to protecting the Arctic was to promote education about it.[78] There was a call to action at every age and for all groups: mandatory learning for policymakers about climate change and science, required training for cruise ship operators, improved capacities of Arctic universities through additional funding, teaching of polar law and policy, and polar science. Quotations capture the sentiment. Summarizing the thoughts of several respondents on the value of education to Arctic sustainability:

> Many people, mostly outside of academia, have no idea what is going on in the Arctic.

What is considered important is the way education is carried out:

> It would be appropriate to offer multidisciplinary courses in "Polar Sciences." For two reasons: 1) to build future generations of polar experts, capable of negotiating the complex new legal and policy arrangements needed in the polar regions and based on the most updated scientific findings; 2) to boost awareness, globally, on the important role played by Poles.
>
> Scientists need to be effective communicators to policy makers and general citizens to make clear not only what their research shows, but why we need certain policies and why it is important to the audience they are addressing (including state legislators, city mayors, oil industry, fishing industry, global and local health policy makers, economists, etc.). The science-policy interface and the science-communication interface are very important.

With regard to the accessibility of good information,

> what is needed is broad scholarship to take better advantage of indigenous knowledge; and partner better with policy makers and other users

> of the scholarship to make academic products more readily accessible and actionable.

And as to what is needed to make knowledge more accepted:

> Train and educate more local, indigenous scientists. Education can be counterproductive as it might be perceived negatively, if Southerners, even if it is based on scientific data, come and tell people in the Arctic what to do. There is a risk that this would be perceived in a paternalistic, colonialist manner—and this will help no-one. Now, if Arctic scientists are trained and educated, and they reach the same conclusions of the scientists of the South or experience good cooperation, then this will probably have a strong effect.

Another related issue:

> I think a major problem of many great research projects is that the important findings are not communicated with decision makers/that potential policy/governance implications are not obvious. I think it would be a great step forward if academia worked more actively with regulatory and communication experts to make sure the research can be used to inform governance.

What needs to be communicated is understood broadly:

> Beyond science, the academic world can contribute economists, artists & writers, psychologists, and others who can contribute to developing and communicating policy. Importantly, when discussing the "academic world" include traditional and indigenous knowledge, both that which has been formally incorporated in the academic world and that which has not.

Education can more fully take place at all levels and for people of all ages. Some school systems incorporate teaching on the environment in general and climate change in particular in their curriculum, including in early grades. Many organizations worldwide dedicate themselves not to making new laws or funding mitigation or adaptation strategies in the Arctic, but to learning more and teaching more about it. Table 4.3 is a sample.

These organizations, and others which do not do their own Arctic research, use and rely on a vast network of Arctic scientific activity. Among the leaders worldwide in creating knowledge, in addition to those in the Arctic nations, are enterprises in Japan, Korea, the UK, Germany and China. Poland also

Table 4.3 Organizations That Focus on Environmental Education about the Arctic

- Northern Forum is a nonprofit organization based in Yakutsk, Sakha Republic (Yakutia). Subnational government leaders from Northern or near Northern countries are brought together to address common political, environmental and economic issues with a major focus on sustainable development. Private interests have membership but not voting status. (https://www.northernforum.org/en/)[a]
- Arctic Institute of North America, University of Calgary, advances knowledge for a changing North. (https://arctic.ucalgary.ca/)
- ArcticNet is a network of centers of excellence of Canada that brings together scientists and managers in the natural, human health and social sciences with partners from Inuit organizations, Northern communities, federal and provincial agencies, and the private sector. (http://www.arcticnet.ulaval.ca/vision-and-mission/about-us)
- Arctic Portal provides access to news, data, information and organizations across the Arctic; facilitates information sharing and cooperation between public and private parties; and carries out Arctic-related outreach and communication. (https://arcticportal.org/about-us)
- Arctic Research Consortium of the United States is an Arctic in the Classroom partnership of scientists, educators and communities. (https://www.arcus.org/tac)
- Circumpolar Conservation Union protects the ecological and cultural integrity of the Arctic by promoting understanding and cooperation among Arctic indigenous peoples, environmental organizations and other interests; raises public awareness of the importance of the Arctic; and advocates policies and institutions that will protect the environment, promote sustainability and respect the human rights of Arctic communities and peoples. (https://circumpolar.org/about/)
- Friends of the Earth/Norges Naturvernforbund, Norway's oldest environmental and nature protection organization, works to strengthen environmental awareness, concern and practice. (https://naturvernforbundet.no/?lang=en_GB)
- International Arctic Research Center fosters Arctic research to help understand, prepare for and adapt to the pan-Arctic impacts of climate change. (https://uaf-iarc.org/about-iarc/)
- International Arctic Science Committee is a nongovernmental international scientific organization that encourages and facilitates cooperation in Arctic research. (https://iasc.info/iasc/about-iasc)
- International Polar Foundation supports polar scientific research for the advancement of knowledge and the promotion of informed action on climate change as well as the development of a sustainable society. (http://www.polarfoundation.org/about)
- National Science Foundation Arctic Research Program works to gain better understanding of the Arctic's biological, geophysical, chemical and sociocultural processes, and the interactions of ocean, land, atmosphere, biological and human systems. (https://www.nsf.gov/geo/opp/arctic/index.jsp)
- National Science Foundation's Arctic Observing Network) funds long-term field observations to detect and understand Arctic system change on long time scales. (https://www.nsf.gov/funding/pgm_summ.jsp?pims_id=503222)
- Scott Polar Research Institute, University of Cambridge, works to enhance the understanding of the polar regions through research and publication and educating new generations of polar researchers, projecting the history and environmental significance of the polar regions to the wider community. (https://www.spri.cam.ac.uk/)

Table 4.3 (continued)

- The Institute of Arctic Studies at the John Sloan Dickey Center for International Understanding acts as a crossroad for interdisciplinary research, discussion and education on global climate change and Arctic policy issues. (https://dickey.dartmouth.edu/arctic-environment/about-institute-arctic-studies)
- University of the Arctic is a network of universities, colleges and other organizations committed to higher education and research in the North to build post-secondary education programs accessible to Northern students. (https://www.uarctic.org/)
- Arctic Funders Collaborative focuses on knowledge exchange, learning opportunities and raising the profile of the Arctic; members are public and private foundations that promote grant making in the Arctic; funding involves locals' participation. (https://www.arcticfunders.com/
- International Arctic Social Sciences Association has the goal to increase the participation of social scientists (broadly interpreted) in national and international Arctic research and promote the collection, exchange, dissemination and archiving of scientific information in the Arctic social sciences. (https://iassa.org/about-iassa/objectives)
- The Polar Institute of the Wilson Center addresses policy issues facing polar regions with emphases on Arctic governance, climate change, economic development, scientific research, security and indigenous peoples. (https://www.wilsoncenter.org/program/polar-institute.[b]

Notes:

[a] Waliul Hasanat, "Searching for Synergies in International Governance Systems Developed in the Circumpolar North," McGill International Journal of Sustainable Development Law and Policy (Revue Internationale De Droit Et Politique Du Développement Durable De McGill), Vol. 9, No. 2 (2013): 5–41, accessed August 13, 2021, http://www.jstor.org/stable/24352641.accessed.

[b] Ogor Osipov, "International Arctic Research: Analyzing Global Funding Trends. A Pilot Report," Digital Science, Report. April 24, 2017, https://doi.org/10.6084/m9.figshare.4829455.v1.

has funded Arctic research projects. Within a decade, 3,000,000 projects with funding totaling $1.1 trillion (US dollars) were identified by investigators.[79] Participating scientists have observed the following:

> While international Arctic research collaboration has existed since the 19th century, irrespective of political conditions, it has grown noticeably over the last two decades through initiatives such as the "International Polar Year" (2007–2008). In the midst of increasing international turmoil, the Arctic has become one of the few transnational arenas for collaboration, discussion, and mutual interest among leading global players. From the earth and life sciences to the arts, humanities, and social sciences the Arctic is truly a highly connected international and interdisciplinary laboratory.[80]

"Scientific diplomacy in the Arctic has been an important part of both Arctic Council successes and other bilateral and multilateral agreements that have helped keep the region peaceful and productive."[81]

Surely there will be setbacks and incidents of scientific secrecy and perhaps even hoarding or corruption of data, but overall the contributions of many nations and their research entities have provided an evolving understanding of the environment and peoples of the Arctic. This has been the case both when Russia and when other Arctic countries have led scientific cooperative activity.

Funding for scientific research and education, civic action and law to protect the Arctic are broadly carried out now. In 50 years, the age of the United Nations oceans programs, as a result of this significant work, will the Arctic be sustaining? Will it be healthier in the senses we have addressed in *Polar Shift*? It very well can be. There are some gaps in each of these influencers, law, learning and giving, but they are not yawning gaps—although some are critical. Chapter 5 addresses how they should be filled.

NOTES

1 Mariano Aupilaarjuk, Marie Tulimaaq, Akisu Joamie, Emile Imaruittuq, and Lucassie Nutaraaluk, "Respect for Wildlife," in Jarich Oosten, Frederic Laugrand, and Willem Rasing (eds), *Inuit Laws* (Iqaluit: Nunavut Arctic College Media, 2017), https://uci.on.worldcat.org/oclc/985966196.

2 Susanne Rust, "A U.S. Tribe Wants to Resume Whale Hunting. Should It Revive This Tradition?," *Los Angeles Times*, December 1, 2009, https://www.latimes.com/environment/story/2019-12-01/whale-hunting-makah-tribe-tradition-washington-state.

3 Here, *rules* encompasses the wide range of formal, even if not written, social actions addressed at protection of the Arctic. This is similar to the definition in the World Ocean Assessment of the United Nations but in a more encompassing way. The United Nations First World Ocean Assessment notes that "the social rules that have developed to control human activities—including national legislation, the law of the sea, international agreements on particular human uses of the sea and broader international agreements that apply to both land and sea" (The First Global Integrated Marine Assessment: World Ocean Assessment I, https://www.un.org/Depts/los/global_reporting/WOA_RPROC/WOACompilation.pdf, p. 4, 2016.) We include norms, practices of indigenous peoples, government policies, education and economics based activities.

4 Kristina Schonfeldt (ed.), *The Arctic in International Law and Policy* (Oxford: Hart Publishing, 2017).

5 Dawn Alexandrea Berry, Nigel Bowles and Halbert Jones (eds.), *Governing the North American Arctic Sovereignty, Security, and Institutions* (New York: Palgrave Macmillan, 2016).

6 Article 21(1)(h) of UNCLOS. See United Nations Convention on the Law of the Sea, part II, section 4, article 33 1(a), https://www.un.org/depts/los/convention_agreements/texts/unclos/unclos_e.pdf (1982).

7 "Sedentary Species," UN Atlas of the Oceans, accessed July 30, 2019, http://www.oceansatlas.org/subtopic/en/c/20/.

8 "United Nations Convention on the Law of the Sea of 10 December 1982," last updated, February 11, 2020, accessed January 15, 2022, Oceans & Law of the Sea, United Nations, https://www.un.org/Depts/los/convention_agreements/convention_overview_convention.htm.

9 Atsuko Kanehara, "The Revenue Sharing Scheme with Respect to the Exploitation of the Outer Continental Shelf under article 82 of the United Nations Convention of the Law of the Sea—A Plethora of Entangled Issues," paper presented in Seminar on the Establishment of the Outer Limits of the Continental Shelf beyond 200 Nautical Miles under UNCLOS, February 27, 2008, accessed 9 June 2020, https://www.spf.org/en/_opri_media/pdf/acb.pdf.

10 The court rejected the application of the principle of equidistance and said that it was not inherent in the basic concept of continental shelf rights. Nor was it a rule of customary international law.

11 Article 63 of the United Nations Convention on the Law of the Sea (hereafter UNCLOS, cited by section/article numbers) notes thus:

> Stocks occurring within the exclusive economic zones of two or more coastal States or both within the exclusive economic zone and in an area beyond and adjacent to it.
>
> 1. Where the same stock or stocks of associated species occur within the exclusive economic zones of two or more coastal States, these States shall seek, either directly or through appropriate subregional or regional organizations, to agree upon the measures necessary to coordinate and ensure the conservation and development of such stocks [...].
> 2. Where the same stock or stocks of associated species occur both within the exclusive economic zone and in an area beyond and adjacent to the zone, the coastal State and the States fishing for such stocks in the adjacent area shall seek, either directly or through appropriate subregional or regional organizations, to agree upon the measures necessary for the conservation of these stocks in the adjacent area. (https://www.un.org/depts/los/convention_agreements/texts/unclos/unclos_e.pdf, accessed January 15, 2022).

12 Article 64 of the UNCLOS:

> Highly migratory species.
>
> 1. The coastal State and other States whose nationals fish in the region for the highly migratory species [...] shall cooperate directly or through appropriate international organizations with a view to ensuring conservation and promoting the objective of optimum utilization of such species throughout the region, both within and beyond the exclusive economic zone. In regions for which no appropriate international organization exists, the coastal State and other States whose nationals harvest these species in the region shall cooperate to establish such an organization and participate in its work. (https://www.un.org/depts/los/convention_agreements/texts/unclos/unclos_e.pdf, accessed January 15, 2022).

13 "Deep Sea Mining," Issues Brief, IUCN, accessed January 15, 2022, https://www.iucn.org/resources/issues-briefs/deep-sea-mining.

14 Senators Kelly Ayotte and Rob Portman were among the opponents to the Law of the Sea Treaty (www.politico.com/story/2012/07/law-of-the-sea-treaty-sinks-in-senate-078568, accessed July 30, 2019).

15 UNCLOS, Preservation of the Marine Environment, section V, articles 204 and ff., https://www.un.org/depts/los/convention_agreements/texts/unclos/unclos_e.pdf (1982).

16 UNCLOS, part XII, section 1, article 194, https://www.un.org/depts/los/convention_agreements/texts/unclos/unclos_e.pdf (1982).

17 UNCLOS, section VIII, article 234, https://www.un.org/depts/los/convention_agreements/texts/unclos/unclos_e.pdf (1982).

18 Jeremy Bender, "2 Countries Have Been Fighting over an Uninhabited Island by Leaving Each Other Bottles of Alcohol for Over 3 Decades," Business Insider, January 10, 2016, accessed June 10, 2020, https://www.businessinsider.in/defense/2-countries-have-been-fighting-over-an-uninhabited-island-by-leaving-each-other-bottles-of-alcohol-for-over-3-decades/articleshow/50523517.cms.

19 Commission on the Limits of the Continental Shelf (CLCS), Purpose, Functions and Sessions, Oceans & Law of the Sea, United Nations, Division for Oceanic Affairs and the Law of the Sea, https://www.un.org/Depts/los/clcs_new/commission_purpose.htm.

20 Commission on Limits of Continental Shelf Concludes Fifty-First Session," UN Meetings Coverage and Press Releases, United Nations, December 2, 2019, accessed January 16, 2022, https://www.un.org/press/en/2019/sea2120.doc.htm.

21 United States Naval Institute News, "Report to Congress on Changes in the Arctic," December 27, 2019, accessed May 15, 2020, https://news.usni.org/2019/12/27/report-to-congress-on-changes-in-the-arctic-4.

22 Submissions, through the Secretary-General of the United Nations, to the Commission on the Limits of the Continental Shelf (CLCS), accessed August 12, 2021, https://www.un.org/depts/los/clcs_new/commission_purpose.htm. Also see The Arctic, in Benjamin J. Sacks et al., "Exploring Gaps in Arctic Governance," RAND Corporation Document Number RR-A1007-1, https://doi.org/10.7249/RR-A1007-1 (2021).

23 Terence Andrew Check, Jr., "Finding the Right Forum: The Need for Novel Multilateral Diplomatic Solutions to Resolve Competing Territorial Claims Over the Arctic's Natural Resources," October 31, 2013, https://www.unclosdebate.org/citation/1897/finding-right-forum-need-novel-multilateral-diplomatic-solutions-resolve-competing.

24 UNCLOS, article 101, https://www.un.org/depts/los/convention_agreements/texts/unclos/unclos_e.pdf (1982).

25 UNCLOS, article 77(40), https://www.un.org/depts/los/convention_agreements/texts/unclos/unclos_e.pdf (1982).

26 Central Arctic Ocean Agreement (hereafter CAOFA), article 13(2), Agreement to Prevent Unregulated High Seas Fisheries in the Central Arctic Ocean, Article 13, https://www.dfo-mpo.gc.ca/international/documents/pdf/EN-CAO.pdf (2018).

27 UN General Assembly, United Nations Declaration on the Rights of Indigenous Peoples: Resolution/adopted by the General Assembly, A/RES/61/295, October 2, 2007, accessed March 11, 2021, https://www.refworld.org/docid/471355a82.html.

28 Declaration of Cooperation in the Barents Euro-Arctic Region Conference of Foreign Ministers in Kirkenes, January 11, 1993, https://www.barentsinfo.fi/beac/docs/459 doc KirkenesDeclaration.pdf.
29 Protocol Agreement from the Statutory Meeting of the Regional Council of the Barents Region (The Euro-Arctic Region), Kirkenes, Norway, January 11, 1993, https://www.barentsinfo.fi/beac/docs/501_doc_StatutoryMeetingRegionalCouncil.pdf.
30 See Barents Euro-Arctic Cooperation, accessed March 3, 2021, https://www.barentscooperation.org/en.
31 The Crown has a duty to consult aboriginal peoples when it has either real or constructive knowledge of an aboriginal right and title and is contemplating action that might affect either the right or title. Risa Schwartz, "Realizing Indigenous Rights in International Environmental Law—A Canadian Perspective," CIGI Paper No. 109, October 12, 2016, accessed November, 2019, https://ssrn.com/abstract=3054146.
32 Survey respondent. See description of the survey in Chapter 1.
33 See the http://www.cites.org/eng/disc/how.php for how CITES works.
34 "6 celebrities Who Condemned Canada's Seal Hunt," CBC Archives, March 15, 2019, last updated March 15, 2019.
35 World Trade Organization, European Communities—Measures Prohibiting the Importation and Marketing of Seal Products, June 8, 2015, DS400, DS401, accessed August 9, 2020, https://www.wto.org/english/tratop_e/dispu_e/cases_e/ds400_e.htm.
36 "Harper Government Responds to WTO Decision on EU Ban on Seal Products," News Release, Government of Canada, May 22, 2014, https://www.canada.ca/en/news/archive/2014/05/harper-government-responds-wto-decision-eu-ban-seal-products.html.
37 "WTO Appellate Body deems EU seal ban 'justified,' implementation flawed," WTO Dispute Settlement, May 27, 2014, https://ictsd.iisd.org/bridges-news/bridges/news/wto-appellate-body-deems-eu-seal-ban-justified-implementation-flawed.
38 Dustin Patar, "An Inuit Exemption to the European Union's Seal Product Ban is Ineffective, a New Report Says," Nunatsiaq News, Artictoday, January 28, 2020, accessed January 28, 2020, https://www.arctictoday.com/an-inuit-exemption-to-the-european-unions-seal-product-ban-is-ineffective-a-new-report-says/.
39 Kristina Schonfeldt, *The Arctic in International Law and Policy* (Oxford: Bloomsbury, 2017).
40 United Nations Envirpnmental Programme (UNEP), The Regional Seas Programmes, accessed May 4, 2020, http://www.unep.org/regionalseas/programmes/, https://perma.cc/4K6X-9SW9.
41 M. Gorbachev's, Speech in Murmansk at the Ceremonial Meeting on the Occasion of the Presentation of the Order of Lenin and the Gold Star to the City of Murmansk, Murmansk, October 1, 1987 (Novosti Press Agency: Moscow, 1987), pp. 23–31, https://www.barentsinfo.fi/docs/gorbachev_speech.pdf.
42 Report of the United Nations Conference on Environment and Development, A/CONF.151/26 (Vol. I), Principle 15, August 12, 1992, https://www.un.org/en/development/desa/population/migration/generalassembly/docs/globalcompact/A_CONF.151_26_Vol.I_Declaration.pdf.

43 See United Nations, Department of Economic and Social Affairs: Sustainable Development, https://sustainabledevelopment.un.org/.
44 The Ilulissat Declaration, May 28, 2008, 48 I.L.M. 362.
45 Ibid.
46 It requires that countries ensure that activity within them does not cause damage to the environment of another state or the global commons.
47 The Nunavut Agreement is available at https://nlca.tunngavik.com/. See Consultation on Nunavut Fishery Regulations: https://www.dfo-mpo.gc.ca/fisheries-peches/consultation/nunavut-eng.html.
48 Several tribunals hear conflicts in or about the Arctic: the International Court of Justice or World Court, the European Court of Human Rights, the European Court of Justice, the Inter-American Court of Human Rights and the Court of Justice of the European Free Trade Association States. Generally in international law, the decisions of courts do not have precedential importance as they do in common law countries but they do have influence—because of their newsworthiness, because of the power of their reasoning, because of the general respect given the judiciary.
49 United States Government Accountability Office, Report to Congressional Requesters, "Alaska Native Villages, Limited Progress Has Been Made on Relocating Villages Threatened by Flooding and Erosion," accessed January 16, 2022, https://digital.library.unt.edu/ark:/67531/metadc301497/m1/1/.
50 According to the Climate Change Center at Columbia University Sabine Center, they have used both state law and federal law and a range of legal arguments. Parties sue based on legislation, federal law such as the Clean Air Act or the National Environmental Policy Act, constitutional claims,state law, common law civil actions as well as creative new arguments.
51 Many cases brought under the federal air quality law have had similar fates; petitions were denied or claims dismissed. Environmentalists have, however, seen some success.
52 Luciano Lliuya v. RWE AG. 2015, Case No. 2 O 285/15, Essen Regional Court.
53 See Barry Kellman, "Climate Change in the Endangered Species Act: A Jurisprudential Enigma," Environmental Law Reporter News and Analysis, Vol. 46 (2016): 10845–46. See also Center for Biological Diversity, "Notice of Violations for Hilcorp's Pipeline Leak in the Cook Inlet, Alaska," February 27, 2017, https://www.biologicaldiversity.org/species/mammals/Cook_Inlet_beluga_whale/pdfs/NOI_Cook_Inlet_Gas_Leak_2017.pdf.
54 Alaska Oil & Gas Ass'n v. Jewell, Circuit Court of Appeals, Alaska Wilderness League v. Jewell, No. 13-35866 (9th Cir., 2015); 815 F 3d 544, 559 (9th Cir., 2014). See also Alaska Oil & Gas Ass'n v. Prizker, 2014 WL 3726121 (D Alaska, July 25, 2014).
55 A decision of the Supreme Court Canada in Clyde River (Hamlet) v. Petroleum Geo-Services Inc., 2017 S.C.C. 4 0 7) 1S.C.R.1069, overturned a Canadian National Energy Board decision. The board had allowed seismic testing relating to oil and gas production in the Arctic Ocean. The Canadian Supreme Court ruled that the board did not properly consult with the Inuit of the area (https://scc-csc.lexum.com/scc-csc/scc-csc/en/item/16743/index.do).
56 Petition to the Inter-American Commission on Human Rights Seeking Relief From Violations Resulting from Global Warming Caused By Acts and Omissions of the

United States, December 7, 2005https://secureservercdn.net/45.40.145.201/hh3.0e7.myftpupload.com/wp-content/uploads/finalpetitionicc.pdf.

57 Petition to the Inter-American Commission on Human Rights Seeking Relief from Violations of the Rights of Arctic Athabaskan Peoples Resulting from Rapid Arctic Warming and Melting Caused by Emissions of Black Carbon by Canada, accessed August 8, 2010, https://climate-laws.org/cclow/geographies/international/litigation_cases/petition-to-the-inter-american-commission-on-human-rights-seeking-relief-from-violations-of-the-rights-of-arctic-athabaskan-peoples-resulting-from-rapid-arctic-warming-and-melting-caused-by-emissions-of-black-carbon-by-canada.

58 Illinois Central Railroad v. Illinois, 146 U.S. 387 (1892).

59 Mary Christina Woo, "You Can't Negotiate with a Beetle": Environmental Law for a New Ecological Age," *Natural Resources Journal*, Vol. 50, No. 102 (2010): 200–202.

60 See, e.g., Juliana v. United States, No. 6:15-cv-01517-TC, 2016, US Dist WL 6661146; Filippone ex rel Filippone v. Iowa Dep't Nat Resources, 829 N W 2d 589; Funk v. Wolf, 144 A 3d 228 (Pa App 2016); Texas Commission Envt'l Quality v. Bonser-Lain, 438 S W 3d 887.

61 Pandey v. India (2017) (National Green Tribunal of India).

62 Urgenda Foundation v. Kingdom of the Netherlands (2015) HAZA C/09/00456689 (Netherlands District Court).

63 Leghari v. Pakistan (2015) WP No. 25501/201(Lahore High Court of Pakistan).

64 Mbabazi et al. v. The Attorney General and National Environmental Management Authority (2012) No. 283 (High Court of Kampala in Uganda).

65 Juliana v. United States, No. 17-71692 (9th Cir., 7 March 2018).

66 Juliana v. United States, No. 18-36082 (9th Cir. January 17, 2020), https://cdn.ca9.uscourts.gov/datastore/opinions/2020/01/17/18-36082.pdf.

67 Case No. 1:16-cv-11950 (D Mass 2016).

68 Adopted by the General Conference of the International Labour Organization, Convention No.169, June 27, 1989.

69 Mathieu Landriault, Andrew Chater, Elana Rowe and P. Lackenbauer, "Civil Society in Arctic Governance," in Mathieu Landriault, Andrew Chater, Elana Wilson Rowe and P. Whitney Lackenbauer (eds.), *Governing Complexity in the Arctic Region* (New York: Routledge, 2020).

70 See text accompanying notes 34–36 above. The rule is Regulation (EC) No. 1007/2009 of the European Parliament and of the Council on trade in seal products (the Basic Regulation), accessed August 31, 2020, https://eur-lex.europa.eu/legal-content/EN/TXT/?uri=CELEX:32009R1007.

71 European Parliament resolution of January 20, 2011, on a sustainable EU policy for the High North (2009/2214(INI), 31, https://eur-lex.europa.eu/legal-content/EN/TXT/?uri=CELEX%3A52011IP0024.

72 See https://arcticwwf.org/work/governance/acscorecard19/, accessed on January 31, 2020.

73 The survey and our methods are described in Chapter 1. The survey question posed was: "Is more international law needed to improve the Arctic environment in the future?"

74 United Nations, *The Second World Ocean Assessment: World Ocean Assessment II* (New York: United Nations, 2021), accessed May 26, 2021, https://www.un.org/regularprocess/sites/www.un.org.regularprocess/files/2011859-e-woa-ii-vol-ii.pdf.

75 See https://www.greengrants.org/where-we-work/north-america/.

76 See https://www.nefco.org/about-nefco/.

77 Guggenheim Partners, "Endorses World Economic Forum's Arctic Investment Protocol," January 21, 2016, https://www.guggenheimpartners.com/firm/news/guggenheim-partners-endorses-world-economic-forums; "Guggenheim Partners announces Arctic investment fund," *The Guardian*, November 16, 2011, https://www.theguardian.com/environment/2011/nov/16/guggenheim-partners-arctic-investment-fund.

78 The question posed is: "Other than law, what other institutions (education, religion, philanthropy, citizen activism [...] others) do you consider important to reaching goals of Arctic environmental protection?"

79 Comment from a very helpful anonymous reviewer of a draft of *Polar Shift*.

80 Ogor Osipov, "International Arctic Research: Analyzing Global Funding Trends. A Pilot Report," Digital Science, Report. April 24, 2017, https://doi.org/10.6084/m9.figshare.4829455.v1.

81 Comment from a very helpful anonymous reviewer of a draft of *Polar Shift*.

5

THE ARCTIC SUSTAINED

"Survive." You use the word "survive." We don't need people to tell us how to survive. This is our life, our home. We have maintained it for centuries; we don't need to be told about survival.[1]

"The Arctic is not in crisis." This is not a headline you will see in *USA Today* or on the cover of *Time* or *National Geographic*. Such "news" is not news: it does not grab a potential reader. Nor is this the conclusion of *Polar Shift*. But the message of analysis of environmental and social conditions and of influencers of sustainability (law, policy, philanthropy, science, education and civil society) is, while cautionary, also optimistic.

CONTINUING CHANGE, COOPERATIVELY ADDRESSED

The Arctic environment will continue to change. Warm temperatures will become common. Threatened and other species will migrate, or try to, from and to the region. Erosion will eat at the coasts of Arctic communities. Glaciers sadly will become smaller. In places, the ocean will be more polluted. Physical changes will lead to political flare-ups and disagreements and skirmishes among nations. These may boil over and even lead to conflict at times.

But the Arctic is no Easter Island, home to the Rapanui who in one, admittedly controversial, historical telling so badly treated their environment that their society went into a downward spiral and declined. The Arctic is not fated to so suffer and disappear as also have other regions described by Jared Diamond in *Collapse*.[2] We are in a different state of knowledge, cultural understanding and commitment to saving places than was the case for previously lost cultures. Among those Diamond described was one in the Arctic. Diamond told the story of the destiny of Vikings who left Norway a 1,000 years ago heading for what would become Greenland. There in a place that today is uninhabitable they found a little part of the world different from the brutally harsh conditions elsewhere on the giant island. There, two colonies prospered—the Eastern and Western Settlements—amid beautiful wildflowers and forests of birch and other trees. As many as 5,000 people lived in what they thought of as a green land. The Norse, rather than learning from the Inuit upon whose lands they had settled, call them *skraelings* ("wretches") and looked down upon them, their food choices and their orientation to the climate and land on which they lived. The new settlers did not learn how to manage the Greenland environment for the long run. They treated it as if it was their original home, the farmlands of southern Norway. Rather than copying Inuit practices for getting fuel (from seal blubber) and food (including ringed seals), they lived as if they had not left their very different homeland. The Norse died of starvation. The Inuit live on in accordance with the climate and land on which they lived.

The lesson of *Collapse* is that "societies, as often as not, aren't murdered. They commit suicide: they slit their wrists and then, in the course of many decades, stand by passively and watch themselves bleed to death."[3] That is not happening in the Arctic, and it need not be so in the future. Nor must we face a future where the non-Arctic does to the region what the Norse did for themselves a millennium ago. We need not mismanage the environment as did the Vikings and the Easter Islanders and others whose civilizations have disappeared.

For the most part, people managing the Arctic environment want to do so cooperatively. Surely they will receive counterdirectives at times from Moscow or Washington or Ottawa. Cyclical tensions will continue. But the interests of indigenous peoples, professional government workers, environmental activists and businesses in the Arctic states remain while political stances oscillate. They can swing back and forth to a more engaged mode; we have seen this with Russia and the United States over time recently in the START and NEW Start discussions on nuclear weapons.[4] Several forces push for ongoing cooperation. People who think of themselves as citizens of the planet want to preserve the beauty, culture and environmental richness of this place. This is true both for Northerners and for those in the non-Arctic who are watching, monitoring and caring. Many also want a peaceful world order that allows some development, including under reasonably strict rules, of the sand and diamonds and reindeer and fish—and some of the oil and gas—of the immense North. If managed well, these vast riches can benefit people of the North and beyond. Strong talents in the region and outside of it have a better understanding of how to protect these resources than was the case years ago when other seas were depleted and when other lands were polluted. Now decisions are guided by strategies for protecting special marine areas, management based on knowledge of how ocean ecosystems work, access to ways of mining that are less energy consuming, recognition of the fact that what is done on land often hurts the waters, technologies that work remotely and so on. Decisions also more and more reflect, at least in part, the views of peoples who will be directly helped or hurt by outcomes and who have known the Arctic for centuries.

FUTURES

A number of forces will generate the future conditions of the Arctic and require continued or increased stewardship. To sum up, among the reasonably likely futures in the Arctic, climate change with its concomitant effects will continue. On average, temperatures will be higher in much of the Arctic. Acidic seas will persist and increase in parts. Both sea and land ice will be less pervasive. So too will snow: there will be less. Considerable land areas will no longer have permafrost, and the effects of thawing will be visible in many regions. But loss of permafrost will have stabilized.[5] Water quality will oscillate, and plastics will arrive in outbursts in the seas. Trees will move further North and will be harmed by newly arrived pests. The great sea mammals will have stable populations. Fisheries will be sustained. The influence of indigenous peoples on law and policy choices will further expand. Erosion will increase, and coastal villages will diminish in size. The ozone layer will be stable. Persistent organic chemicals will continue to threaten forms of life. Human populations—seasonal, permanent and newly permanent—will grow.

For some conditions, we know a bit more.

Tourism. The number of visitors to Arctic nations will continue to increase despite cycles caused by economic downturns and world health crises. But tourism will be more managed. Arctic residents are slowly beginning to understand that more people visiting their wonderful lands is not an unalloyed good. Arctic nations, like Italian regions and parts of Africa and South America—although slowly and often with considerable opposition—can limit large cruise ships, set numerical limits on visits to vulnerable sites and ban plastics sales. And they can restrict giant tourist bus access to core areas, charge for entries that were once free, provide low polluting buses and trams and trains and avoid worldwide marketing. (How does one stop, however, a *New York Times* piece on "the top most beautiful places to visit that no one knows about"?) Some limits come also from the market: the high costs of visiting Arctic places and the absence of infrastructure in the more remote destinations, the disappointment of encountering crowds of people eating Doritos and sipping beer instead of enjoying views of polar bears or beautiful lagoons.

Fossil fuel extraction. It is unlikely that movements to "keep it all in the ground" and switch to 100 percent renewable energy sources will end oil and gas exploration, drilling and exploiting activity in the Arctic. But rich sources of fuels, both conventional and renewable, in other parts of the world will slow the pace of demand. So too will investment choices by major institutional buyers. Steps to improve practices in the industry are also having a positive effect. What's more, the Arctic remains a hostile natural environment for the fossil fuel business.

There will be energy demands and production however; as to how much this will be depends on relations between Arctic nations and countries seeking massive amounts of energy. Iceland and China are an example of such a pair. Even there, market cycles and political strains have stalled actual commercial production.[6] And the world is watching as steps are taken to open up oil and gas field exploration off the Arctic, as President Trump's administration did in the Arctic National Wildlife Refuge in Alaska, and which President Biden later suspended.[7]

Shipping passage. It will remain the case for some time that transit of large volumes of cargo worldwide will not be through the Arctic. The Northern Sea Route, while shorter, must compete with more accessible routes through the Suez Canal and the Mediterranean Sea. These passages are fairly precisely charted and have infrastructure that makes them safe and relatively reliable. Also, melting ice in the Arctic shipping routes in its broken-up forms poses dangers to movements by giant ships. Buildup of icebreakers and demand for tourism in Russia and other Arctic nations in the region will nonetheless make for additional ship movements along parts of the Northern routes.

More contingent outcomes

In the longer run, there are outcomes that are even more uncertain. Abrupt massive warming and melting—considered unlikely extreme events as recently as the early part of this century—are no longer science fiction. Accidents of insufficiently prepared cruise and commercial ships can create local and even regional marine pollution from oil spills and waste dumping. Invasive species can wipe out whole fisheries as was done by a jellyfish in the Black Sea in the early 1980s.

This summary is in the absence of significant new influencers (effective new laws, major financial contributions, targeted science and education and civil society actions). It assumes that follow through on complying with existing rules will take place. It further depends on political commitment to Arctic sustainability remaining at least the same.

No doubt, there are other possible futures. Should cooperation be replaced with competition among the world's richest and most consumptive and hungry nations, military conflict might cause considerable environmental damage and disrupt traditional practices. Russia might see nationalism as the way forward. Its territory in the Arctic is huge, and it can pursue its own national interests in possibly very profitable ways while working outside of the Arctic institutions, as well of course as within them. And even Arctic nations that traditionally emphasize scientific and environmental cooperation experience political shifts, at least for a time, that make for great uncertainty about regional relations. The US-Russia case is a particularly volatile one: allies at times in history, bitter enemies for decades and now the unpredictable period of recent years under the Bush, Clinton, Obama, Trump and Biden presidencies and the Putin prime ministries and presidencies. However tension is not limited to the interactions between these two great powers. Finland, Sweden, Norway and some NATO countries recognize the destabilizing influences on Arctic cooperation that come from several Russian actions such as, in the words of NATO, "provocative military activities near NATO's borders stretching from the Baltic to the Black Sea; irresponsible and aggressive nuclear rhetoric, military posture and underlying posture; and the nerve agent attack in the United Kingdom in March 2018, which was a clear breach of international norms."[8]

Now the major Asian nations promote Arctic harmony and that should continue. Asian nations want to be seen as leaders in a very visible theater for international prestige. But it is possible that non-Arctic nations will break from cooperation and try to assert dominance in the region out of desperation for resources, seeking greater influence on the world stage or for commercial reasons.

Possible futures, those seen as improvements and those that bring dire predictions, are also linked to the pace of economic growth. Is the Arctic a soon to explode economic market? Its home countries are world powerhouses in the global economy, so the question is whether the Arctic parts of these countries will see benefits. In *Is the Arctic an Emerging Market*, the authors concluded that the Arctic is an area in early stages of transition located inside stable, highly developed economies.[9] Put another way, overall, the Arctic Eight may thrive at the same time that their most Northern residents see more difficult circumstances. Capitals of nations do not always focus on the needs of those remote in time and space. And centralized decisions in the Arctic often do not reflect deep understandings of what Northerners need or want.

If economic development conditions do prove favorable in the Far North, pressures on the natural environment will accelerate. Will growth equate with environmental degradation? This is a classic question in the economics of the environment: does economic expansion lead to deterioration in air and water quality, and on land through toxic pollution and failure to manage waste? Overall, the nuanced answer, and one that would apply in the Arctic North, is made graphic by envisioning the inverted U-shaped curve that economists use. Early growth leads to environmentally degrading activity. Later, further growth is accompanied by greater environmental understanding, greater capacity to address the downsides of expansion through technology and other means: a move toward better environmental quality. The curve varies with conditions and may be a somewhat different shape in the Arctic North. Arctic nations have committed to protecting their farthermost places. Advances in and sharing of technology—such as in offshore and maritime transport industries and in oil and gas exploration—and cooperation in science could flatten the first parts of the curve, that is, minimize environmental damage. More fossil fuel industrial activity can occur without major reductions in local and regional environmental quality. This leaves aside the broader critical perspective of the global outcome. In at least some Arctic nations, there will be considerable pressure to let the improving quality of life of their own people overcome the advantages globally of curtailing the fossil fuel industry. Sustainability for locals including the poorer and indigenous peoples may be a higher goal.

Then there is an ideal: sustainability in the region deriving from a green economy. Some see the Arctic as a pilot for this vision: society balancing economic growth with environmental protection. The green economy rewards entrepreneurship and innovation in renewable energy sources and measures success with indicators other than traditional gross domestic product. The strategy moves away from entrenched industrial commitments. Its advocates describe new technologies and processes that can be rolled out more easily in the Arctic than in places with established industry leader influence. Among the emphases are the following: in waste processing, in what is called a circular economy, in products reused and recycled. Green economies call for the development of biofuel engineering, including in the Arctic using reindeer breeding waste through processes that are similar to those used for other animals. Ironically, other forms of renewable production, including wind power, may be threats to reindeer life and ways of living among indigenous people.[10] Improving land management patterns, including forest reproduction, is another element of the package of changes.[11] Several sectors in the Arctic are good candidates for processes that provide for sustainability. The diamond company De Beers is an example. It plans to build a "diamond mine of the future" in Nunavut not far northeast of Iqaluit. "We want something that's small, modular and leaves a minimal impact [...] moveable and powered by clean energy." It is part of "FutureSmart mining," which aims to be an industry model for sustainability. Digital technologies also can lessen energy demands: certain parts of work in the mines could be done remotely using new fiber optic-based internet connections, as in the diamond case from Iqaluit. Mines may not even need roads running to them; at least this is the publicized position.

Some future needs are independent of whether environmental change in the Arctic is stable or extreme. The Arctic and those many places in the world that the Arctic influences already need to adapt to sea level rise, temperature increases, permafrost thawing and the other ongoing changes described earlier. Likely, for the Arctic itself putting houses on stilts and other ad hoc efforts will not be enough. Governments will have to move whole communities and villages. They will need to integrate people immigrating because of climate change: those going North for opportunity (relief from intense heat and human rights violations on the one hand, while seeking jobs in the energy and tourism sectors on the other); those leaving states and provinces and territories because of absence of opportunity (e.g., traditional ways of hunting and fishing threatened).

MORE TO BE DONE

To achieve a sustainable future environment of the Arctic, what remains to be done? Who should be doing what now? What leadership activities are needed? Is it time for some modest initiatives ... or new grand schemes? And led by whom? It is no surprise in light of competing interests in the Arctic that answers are not widely shared.

We begin with rules: the law. Here, Arctic followers agree on some actions but not on all. We asked the expert group: "Is more international environmental law needed to improve the Arctic environment in the future?" In the aggregate, a significant number said yes.[12] However, strong opinions run contrary to these views—vehemently among some:

- "Absolutely not."
- "Nature doesn't care about our laws."
- "We don't need more laws, we need an incentive for nations to agree and support the agreements that we have."
- "Local ordinances in Alaska and Canada are adequate, and Russia won't accept international jurisdiction. Therefore, the notion of international organizations having control is just a way to take power from the local people and give it to international elites."

Many, however, conclude that some initiatives need to be taken. They are among people committed to the Arctic who, in rule making and policy forums, political conversations, articles in the popular and local media, and in academic journals favor some important changes.

Future rules

1. Protect the Central Arctic Ocean

No matter what decisions are made on the extent of the outer reaches of the continental shelves of Arctic countries, up to 2 million square kilometers (777,200 square miles) of the Arctic will still not be covered because they are beyond the zoning of the seas under UNCLOS.[13] The surface of the sea, the water below it and the bed of the sea make up a gigantic area needing more attention to the environment. These bits of Areas Beyond National Jurisdiction, including those in the Arctic called the donut hole and the peanut hole, remain places where existing law does not fully reach.[14] These are also places of historically unprecedented fisheries collapse such as of the pollock in the 1980s. Options as to next steps for wisely managing these far ocean areas include activity through the Law of the Sea regime. Here, the increasingly relevant International Seabed Authority, the organization established to manage mineral resources, has made some efforts for environmental protection such as in requiring environmental assessments of activities done in the Area.[15] Also, the widely praised Central Arctic Ocean Fisheries Agreement (CAOFA), described in Chapter 4, aims to prevent unregulated fishing in the high seas portion of the Central Arctic Ocean through the application of precautionary measures. While the agreement will automatically renew unless one of its parties objects, making it permanent before its possible sunset in 16 years can further ensure sustainability of an important sector of Arctic life: fisheries which will become more exploitable with sea ice melt and development of ever more sophisticated fishing means.

Beyond fisheries, more comprehensive coverage remains lacking. So, many countries are actively working for a global treaty on the conservation and sustainable use of marine biodiversity in this area.[16] The treaty will promote the "conservation and sustainable use" of marine resources and living organisms in the high seas, an expanse encompassing 50 percent of the planet's surface and all the water below. These riches can belong to anyone, everyone or no one depending on what rules are made. The stakes are high both for environmental protection and for creation of wealth. These areas are home to deep-sea coral fields. They are also a place where carbon is stored through phytoplankton; fisheries abound; and where yet to be discovered genetic resources exist (i.e., valuable material from plants, animals and microbes that need to be sustained to maintain the complexity of life and which also can be used for human products). The treaty would create special areas of high seas marine protection, develop a means of sharing benefits from the resources and require environmental studies before actions are taken. As of summer 2021, the UN meetings to go forward with a treaty were ongoing but postponed because of the pandemic. An alternative, either if this process fails or until it is completed, could be a regional agreement among the Arctic states for the greater protection of this area.

2. *Protect culture*

Over its now mature life, as described earlier, the law has evolved to consider not only flora and fauna and critters and plants. The law now also seeks to protect cultural traditions, ways of living and artifacts including sacred sites. But important gaps exist in the rules and how they are enforced. With regard to places and artifacts, custodians of indigenous and other special places are stymied for many reasons. Infrastructure construction does not always recognize the existence or importance of sites deeply revered by indigenous people or later settlers. Meaningful consultations can be seen as slowing economic development. There is abuse through nonmanaged tourism or exploitation of cultural treasures. Excessive numbers of visitors arrive and souvenir shops and restaurants and bars replace the serenity of what has been there for millennia.[17] Meanwhile, the erosive and destructive actions of climate change continue to harm these cherished resources. New approaches need to be created. These can come from interpretations and applications of customary law, such as the Precautionary Principle. Also, international human rights law such as the Declaration on the Rights of Indigenous Peoples can be used to protect the cultural value to indigenous people which properly understood is value to all humankind.[18]

3. *Regulate offshore energy installations and assign liability*

As Arctic sea ice melts, more opportunities follow for exploration and exploitation of fossil fuels and for renewables, which in various parts of the Arctic include hydropower, wind, solar, tidal movements, geothermal and nuclear.[19] Careful management will limit damage to sea life, the waters and coastal communities. But where it is absent, where negligence or even intentional actions or unforeseen circumstances lead to pollution, death, damage or destruction, there is a need to identify who should pay and undertake repairs and remediation.

Current laws that address what must be done and who is liable are limited in reach, and across the Arctic countries they are not the same. More developed rules on civil liability are needed—for oil pollution, accidents, disasters and even for common activities such as discharges of bunker oil.[20] Which activities, businesses and professions in which territories deserve compensation for various forms of loss need to be determined. The stakes are high but so too are the challenges of developing fair and effective rules. Several major catastrophic spills, including in the Arctic, make urgent the need for increasing the deterrent effect of rules and improving policies to help those who are victims in a timely manner.

In the Arctic, extreme conditions make for both additional risks of accidents and spills and difficulties of clean up. In the US Arctic, the *Exxon Valdez* case is an iconic example. In 1989, the tanker *Exxon Valdez* ran aground in Alaska's Prince William Sound spilling about 11 million gallons of oil and causing massive environmental damage. It harmed over 1,300 miles of Alaska's coastline. After years of litigation, payments in the hundreds of millions (rather than the originally awarded billions of dollars) were awarded to those harmed by the spill. Also in the Arctic, in 2020, Russian President Putin ordered a Russian company to pay almost $2 billion for a diesel fuel spill of 20,000 tons outside of the city of Norilsk. The amount was contested by the company but was paid. In general, with regard to contemplating new rules in the Arctic, expecting a strong leader like Russia's president to be the enforcer of environmental violations cannot be the norm. A liability regime for the exceptional Arctic region, rather than a patchwork relying on variable court outcomes which may not be reached for years, or shifting political positions by governments—while elusive—should be a goal.

The Deepwater Horizon Gulf of Mexico spill highlighted the complexity of creating effective liability rules. In 2010, 5 million barrels of oil spilled in the Gulf of Mexico in a month-long disaster with continuing damages when a well head blew out. Vexing questions in an unprecedented set of legal actions had to be addressed following the explosion: What amounts of compensation are fair? Who is responsible for what percentages of the losses (there were several defendants including BP, the rig operator and the contractor)? How far in the chain of causation should compensation reach (what is a reasonable cost)? Surely loss of life must be compensated. Recreational losses, employment losses and medical claims also need to be addressed. For example, should restaurants in faraway states be compensated because they lost revenue from the depletion of sea food from the spill? In all, in the Gulf case damages were enormous for loss of life, of environmental resources and business venues, and the liability was both civil and criminal for various actors totaling in the billions of dollars. Questions of liability are made even more vexing on the Arctic High Seas where conditions are at times extremely dangerous.

4. Incorporate indigenous knowledge

People who live in the Arctic often have a different understanding of the scale and nature of a phenomenon than those who study it with models, other peoples' data and site visits. This is true for a range of Arctic concerns, whether they be coastal village erosion or seal or whale hunting. Using the perspectives of learning from organized science and from indigenous experience, observations and study is called joint knowledge production. It has been done well and it has been done poorly.[21] An example of the latter, described in Chapter 3, occurred in the case of trying to understand the 2013 collapse of the reindeer population in the Russian Arctic in 2013–14.[22] When interactions are not positive, joint knowledge attempts can create even greater distance between government and academic scientists on the one hand and indigenous people on the other. Specific rules and those on processes (environmental impact procedures, citizen participation forms and the make-up of work groups) need to better recognize and support involvement of indigenous people, incorporating their views, perspectives and experiences as equal contributors to decision making. Another level of consultation is international, going beyond national obligations (such as the Canadian duty to consult on decisions that could interfere with domestic, aboriginal or treaty rights). New obligations should include a legal requirement to include indigenous peoples in negotiating international environmental agreements and rules on indigenous peoples' human rights.[23]

Other new rules?

What more needs to be done in making rules to sustain the Arctic? Some Arctic experts and leaders advocate special Arctic law on a variety of additional topics. The list is long: create binding rules for Arctic oil and gas exploitation and for shipping emissions; manage more effectively ship ballast water and fuel content; create an active United Nations Regional Seas Programme that can foster treaties as needs are identified as well as designate places (called Particularly Sensitive Sea Areas) in the Arctic to be protected by special actions.

Further action points include the need to identify additional areas for marine protection, adopt treaties that aim to protect a particular threatened species such as the beluga whale and practice ecosystem-based management. Ecosystem-based management is an approach that considers both the physical and social elements of sustainable actions. Variously understood, it is nonetheless strongly and widely advocated by many Arctic experts. In short, it is "the place-based, comprehensive assessment and management of ecosystem impacts," including those of humans—in maintaining environmental quality of large Arctic marine areas.[24] Also on the list is to adopt a comprehensive environmental protection treaty for zones of the Arctic within the jurisdiction of individual countries.

Regarding the Arctic Council, some advocate adding additional members to it, including the near-Arctic nations and those that are capable of commerce through the Arctic Ocean and of exploitation of its resources both on land and in the sea. Other recommendations would remove any distinction between Permanent Participants and members of the Arctic Council. The aim is to make indigenous groups truly equal partners in Arctic Council activities. Some also think the Arctic Council should be changed to make it more of a management and rule-making entity.

As the scourge of plastics so quickly arrived, likely other unforeseen threats will come to the Arctic. To prepare for these, institutions need to be strengthened to be able to respond effectively to evolving crises. Ideally, they would continuously collect information that relates to important trends, assign tasks of anticipating various futures and decentralize their activities so that time can be saved by circumventing the need to bring decisions to a single source. These new governance types would share understandings with institutions in other regions that face the same new threats. The coronavirus pandemic demonstrated the need for this characteristic worldwide.[25] Precaution and preparation can be their hallmarks. Management strategies are numerous and praised in theory. Actual application is less common. But they exist and can apply to Arctic local, regional, bi-national and pan-Arctic agencies.

Geoengineering. In this period of unprecedented Arctic melting and thawing, considerations about sustainability of the environment and Arctic cultures include a topic, until not too long ago, so controversial that friends of the Arctic could not discuss it reasonably: geoengineering. A four-letter word among environmental change activists, geoengineering is manipulation of processes that control environmental change which aim to minimize its negative effects.

Types of geoengineering, described and graphically portrayed in sci-fi fashion, should remain that: fiction. They can create unforeseen harms unimagined by the proponents; they are too risky and carried out only by rogues or renegades. Yet some thoughtful advocates of some types of geoengineering see them not as mad science but as inevitable in light of the pace and impacts of climate change. They conclude that types of engineering can be part of the policy mix (depending on how one defines geoengineering, it already is).

Often noted geo techniques are several. As for climate change, they tend to focus either on removing carbon dioxide (CO_2) from the atmosphere or increasing the amount of sunlight reflected by Earth.[26] Techniques offered include sending craft into space to orbit mirrors; lofting balloons with sulfates into the atmosphere (which has a cooling effect similar to volcanic eruptions); using glass microspheres that act a bit like snow to slow down melting;[27] spraying seawater into the air to form clouds that reflect sunlight and cool the planet;[28] fertilizing the water with iron which speeds up the growth of phytoplankton and thus takes up CO_2; and removing carbon dioxide from the atmosphere and isolating (burying) it on land, in the sea or beneath the sea floor. In parts of the Arctic, to reflect radiation, sand could be used to cover certain types of ice. At least some of these geo interventions are generally what opponents picture and fear and consider morally unacceptable and reckless. A number of these techniques have already been tried, some without guidance by government rules. There are and will also be "soft" geoengineering techniques; simple tree planting is considered an example. In addition to climate change, more generally understood, geoengineering addresses other components of Arctic sustainability: loss or invasion of species, coastal erosion and expansion of the ozone hole.

Knowledge of what some forms of geoengineering will do is very limited. In 2016, a United Nations expert group addressed the potential ecological and social impacts of marine-geoengineering approaches to advise the International Maritime Organization (IMO) and parties to the London Convention and Protocol. The experts concluded that "the evidence trail was so poor. In the end, all we could do was to classify marine geoengineering research as either too insufficient or incomplete to inform a scientific assessment."[29]

The controversial nature of geoengineering divides researchers and policymakers. But researchers should not be the arbiters of which if any of these processes and technologies can be tried. These must be legal conclusions. From the perspective of *Polar Shift*, the focus is on rules on how geoengineering is done, how it is managed without conclusions of whether forms of geoengineering should be pursued—rules that will guide policymakers and who those people and agencies should be. Among the new rules generally advocated to promote Arctic sustainability is a mandate to undertake environmental studies for more cases of development activity; this is a recommendation of many Arctic experts. Its specific application to geoengineering can help move the discussion of whether these interventions, or some of them, have a place in promoting Arctic sustainability.

Geoengineering projects should go through proper government-led environmental review. If approved, careful observations must follow to decide whether the geoengineering actions help or need to be reversed if side effects become too troubling. Whether a technique can be pursued with precaution or generates spiraling harms will vary. Monitoring and control, including by governments and local people most likely to feel the results of these experiments, should be part of the geoengineering cycle. Environmental impact assessment, variously called EIS or EA, is common now in one form or another in decision making regarding development, whether for projects or proposed programs. Simply, it requires that before actions that "significantly affect the quality of the human environment" (the words of many environmental assessment rules) are taken, decision makers must undertake a number of analyses: they need to look before they leap. They need to generate alternative solutions to the proposal with a focus on its goals (in our case, for example, limiting ice melt in the Arctic) and study their impacts. Policymakers need to consult those who might be affected (in many different ways). A lead decision maker, often a government agency, must be designated to conduct the process; this is the case because for many developments several government agencies have roles and interests in promoting, denying or regulating projects. Environmental assessment is very familiar and routine in many parts of the world today under national and international law.[30] It should be strictly required for geoengineering proposals.

Other vehicles exist for developing rules to address geoengineering. National environmental and technology assessment rules; the London Convention and Protocol, which provides a framework for evaluating the evidence for geoengineering approaches; and some other treaties are all potential opportunities to consider what goods or bads a geo process might lead to. For example, signatories of the UN Convention on Biological Diversity voluntarily placed a moratorium on some ocean iron fertilization experiments conducted without proper assessments and which had no controls.[31] And international environmental law and the Law of the Sea both contain general principles that can be used to direct assessment of proposed geotechnologies. If restrictions under these legal instruments are not sufficient, soft law principles (the precautionary principle, the polluter pays) are sufficiently flexible to be employed by opponents of a risky technology. Political action and actions through civil society remain to address particularly perilous or uncertain initiatives.

Views on the need for new rules and approaches for Arctic sustainability differ, for some considerably. What seems clear is that the shorter list, laid out above, will be helpful and is itself ambitious. We have seen that a giant inventory of rules has been made, but to write them down is not enough. A focus on implementation, including through agreements among the Arctic states, is central.

OTHER THAN RULES

It is the law that will further help sustain the Arctic. But law cannot on its own meet that goal. Law is important; it is not enough. Fundamental is the understanding that comes through education—about the strengths and vulnerability of the Arctic, about its history (both human and natural), as well as about how it has changed and is continuing to change in an accelerated way.

Following the pushes from law and a desire for the kind of action that science and science-based education fosters, other influencers will assist to have precaution prevail: corporate responsibility, philanthropy and political action (civil society and formal) which fuel human behavior in this unique and special place.

Finally

The Arctic need not be romanticized to be treasured. It is a place of important physical changes that affect the globe, of long vital cultures, of needed natural resources (sand, energy sources, water, minerals, etc.), of outstanding beauty. It is a setting of wonderful sights. People chat among themselves in timeless languages. They hunt and carve and fish and learn and pray as they have for centuries. Dirt roads extend to what seems to be forever—with not another human, and in places not even an animal, in sight. Water coming from sky-high mountains tumbles to grounds surrounded by brilliant yellow fields dotted and laced with dark black lava. Groups sip drinks by candlelight, outside, at midnight, their laps covered with mammal skins. Skies dance magically in stunning shades of purple and red. Giant herds of caribou march somewhere. Majestic spired wooden churches stand out alone in the horizon. Children skateboard as soon as the ice melts a bit, next to sleek cement and glass buildings where entrepreneurs gather. Scientists work in remote international research stations, white domes which they reach by air or sled working near and with long-time residents.

In the Arctic, it is easy to feel a special attraction, a deep feeling of wanting to protect. Arctic and non-Arctic people now, our children and grandchildren later, should be able to enjoy the cold; to hunt and fish; to feel and play in the snow; to breathe fresh air, clean in a way that makes your lungs almost ache;

to drink melting water, which was minutes ago a glacier; to see whales dancing, seals, and bears up close; to chat with artists sculpting traditional beauty out of stone; to study and save at least part of a cold culture; to pet a reindeer and feel its throbbing soft antlers; and to learn and thrive.

The Arctic will be sustained, its environment even cleaner, its people healthier when people are more engaged with the larger world—a world more understanding of the rights and needs of native peoples, of new migrants, of the harms done in the name of improvement, a world better aware of good science. The Arctic can be richer in all ways as people continue to work to protect a global treasure.

NOTES

1 Indigenous leader at forum on Arctic sustainability reacting to a participant's comment on security in the Arctic. Northern Sustainable Development Forum, Yakutsk, Siberia Russia, 26 September 2019.

2 Jared Diamond, *Collapse: How Societies Choose to Fail or Succeed* (New York: Penguin, 2005). Diamond's views on Easter Island have not gone unchallenged. See Thomas Garlinghouse, "Sapiens Rethinking Easter Island's Historic Collapse," Scientific American, May 30, 2020, accessed August 11, 2020, https://www.scientificamerican.com/article/rethinking-easter-islands-historic-collapse/.

3 Malcolm Gladwell, "The Vanishing," December 26, 2004, New Yorker, https://www.newyorker.com/magazine/2005/01/03/the-vanishing-2.

4 Madeleine Albright & Igor Ivanov, "A Plea to Save the Last Nuclear Arms Treaty," New York Times, February 10, 2020, https://www.nytimes.com/2020/02/10/opinion/albright-ivanov-nuclear-treaty.html.

5 If nations comply with the Paris Agreement, permafrost thawing should be stabilized after the mid-2000s with significant decreases in global greenhouse gas emissions. Key Indicators of Arctic Climate Change 1971–2017.

6 "Stumbling Block: China-Iceland Oil Exploration Reaches an Impasse," Over the Circle, January 24, 2018, accessed March 5, 2020, https://overthecircle.com/2018/01/24/stumbling-block-china-iceland-oil-exploration-reaches-an-impasse/.

7 "Alaska: Biden to Suspend Trump Arctic Drilling Leases," BBC News, June 2, 2021, accessed July 12, 2021, https://www.bbc.com/news/world-us-canada-57322511.

8 "Relations with Russia," NATO, April 21, 2021, accessed July 12, 2021, https://www.nato.int/cps/en/natolive/topics_50090.htm.

9 Maxwell C. McGrath-Horn and Ryan R. Uljua, "Is the Arctic an Emerging Market?," 2018, accessed August 21, 2020, https://arcticyearbook.com/images/yearbook/2018/Scholarly_Papers/2_AY2018_McGrath-Horn.pdf.

10 Melissa Breyer, "Norway Decides in Favor of Wild Reindeer Over Energy," Treehugger, October 11, 2018, accessed August 12, 2021, https://www.treehugger.com/norway-decides-favor-wild-reindeer-over-energy-4848915.

11 "The Arctic May Become Pilot Region for Green Economy," The Arctic, June 9, 2020, https://arctic.ru/economics/20200609/946783.html.

12 About the UCI Arctic Expert Survey, see Chapter 1. Once again, the responses are suggestive and not presented as statistically significant, but here the balance was rather striking despite strong commentary that more law was not needed, nor helpful:

146/203	72%	Yes
32/203	16%	No
25/203	12%	I don't know
		# of responses to this question
2/205	1%	No answer selected

13 Stewart M. Patrick, "Why the U.N. Pact on High Seas Biodiversity Is Too Important to Fail," World Politics Review, July 8, 2019, https://www.worldpoliticsreview.com/articles/28011/why-the-u-n-pact-on-high-seas-biodiversity-is-too-important-to-fail.

14 As laid out in Chapter 3.

15 UNCLOS, article 145.

16 Vito De Lucia, "The BBNJ Negotiations and Ecosystem Governance in the Arctic," Marine Policy, December 18, 2019, accessed September 3, 2020, https://www.sciencedirect.com/science/article/pii/S0308597X19306025.

17 Leena Heinamaki and Thora Martina Herrmann, Experiencing and Protecting Sacred Natural Sites of Sámi and Other Indigenous Peoples: The Sacred Arctic (New York: Springer, 2017).

18 Sophie Starrenburg, "Cultural Heritage Protection: a Truly 'Global' Legal Problem.?, Völkerrechtsblog, September 5, 2018, accessed August 12, 2020, https://voelkerrechtsblog.org/de/cultural-heritage-protection-a-truly-global-legal-problem/. And see George Nicholas, "Protecting Heritage Is a Human Right," The Conversation, September 9, 2018, accessed August 13, 2020, https://theconversation.com/protecting-heritage-is-a-human-right-99501.

19 Magnus de Will, Hlynur Stefansson and Agust Valfells, *Energy Security in the Arctic: Policies and Technologies for Integration of Renewable Energy*, https://arcticyearbook.com/arctic-yearbook/2019/2019-briefing-notes/329-energy-security-in-the-arctic-policies-and-technologies-for-integration-of-renewable-energy, last accessed July 31, 2010.

20 Elizabeth A. Kirk," Science Based Governance and Regulation of Arctic Energy Installations," Arctic Yearbook 2018, https://arcticyearbook.com/images/yearbook/2018/Scholarly_Papers/14_AY2018_Kirk.pdf. See also Beatrice Schutte, "Marine Pollution in the Arctic Region: What Future of Civil Liability?—The Need for a Comprehensive Liability Scheme," in Patrick Chaumette (ed.) *Transforming the Ocean Law by Requirement of the Marine Conservation* (Madrid: Marcial Pons Ediciones Jurídicas y Sociales, S.A., 2019).

21 UN Human Rights Office of the High Commissioner, "Finland/Indigenous Peoples: New Bill Threatens Sami's Rights to Their Traditional Lands and Livelihood," December 17, 2015, accessed August 13, 2020, https://www.ohchr.org/EN/NewsEvents/Pages/DisplayNews.aspx?NewsID=16897.

22 Alexey O. Pristupa et al., "Reindeer Herders Without Reindeer, The Challenges of Joint Knowledge Production on Kolguev Island in the Russian Arctic," SocIety and Natural Resources (November 9, 2018): 338–56. See also S. Kirchner, and V. M. Frese, "Sustainable Indigenous Reindeer Herding as a Human Right," *Laws*, Vol. 5, No. 24 (2016).

23 Risa Schwartz, "Realizing Indigenous Rights in International Environmental Law - A Canadian Perspective," CIGI Paper 109, October 12, 2017, SSRN: https://ssrn.com/abstract=3054146.

24 UC Irvine School of Law, Center for Land, Environment, and Natural Resources (CLEANR), "Advancing Ecosystem-Based Marine Management in the Arctic: Recommendations to the Arctic Council Task Force on Arctic Marine Cooperation," September 2016, accessed February 8, 2022, https://www.law.uci.edu/centers/cleanr/Advancing_EBM_Arctic_Report_CLEANR.pdf.

25 Donald Michael, "On Learning to Plan and Planning to Learn" (New York: Jossey-Bass, 1973). See also J. B. Ruhl, "Regulation by Adaptive Management—Is it Possible?," *Minnesota Journal of Law, Science & Technology*, Vol. 7, No. 21 (2005), https://scholarship.law.umn.edu/mjlst/vol7/iss1/5; James Oglethorpe, *Adaptive Management: From Theory to Practice*, Sui Technical Series (Switzerland and Cambridge, UK: IUCN, 2002).

26 L. Miller, , F. Fripiat, S. Moreau, D. Nomura, J. Stefels, N. Steiner, L. Tedesco and M. Vancoppenolle, "Implications of Sea Ice Management for Arctic Biogeochemistry," *Eos*, Vol. 101 (2020), September 30, 2020, https://doi.org/10.1029/2020EO149927. The IPCC, the Intergovernmental Panel on Climate Change, has concluded that to limit warming to 1.5°C compared to pre-industrial levels, perhaps 20 billion tons (gigatonnes) of CO_2 annually need to be removed from the atmosphere for the next several decades.

27 Ice911, a nonprofit group, has begun research to "prove to the world that we can preserve and restore Arctic ice" (see Arctic Ice Project https://www.ice911.org/).

28 Philomene Verlaan, "Geo-engineering, the Law of the Sea, and Climate Change," *Carbon & Climate Law Review*, Vol. 3, No. 4 (2009): 13, https://doi.org/10.21552/CCLR/2009/4/115. See also Albert Lin, "Avoiding Lock-In of Solar Geoengineering," *Northern Kentucky Law* Review, Vol. 47, No. 2 (2020), UC Davis Legal Studies Research Paper Forthcoming, https://ssrn.com/abstract=3797329.

29 Philip Boyd and Chris Vivian, "Should We Fertilize Oceans or Seed Clouds? No One Knows," *Nature*, Vol. 570, No. 7760 (June 11, 2019), https://www.nature.com/articles/d41586-019-01790-7.

30 Daniel Bodansky and Hugh Hunt, "Arctic Climate Interventions," *International Journal of Marine and Coastal Law*, Vol. 35 (2020): 596–617, https://ssrn.com/abstract=3657284.

31 Jeff Tollefson, "UN Decision Puts Brakes on Ocean Fertilization," *Nature*, Vol. 453, No. 704 (June 3, 2008), https://doi.org/10.1038/453704b.

INDEX

ARCTIC REGION
North Pacific Ocean
ALEUTIAN ISLANDS
Bering Sea
KURIL ISLANDS
JAPAN
Petropavlovsk-Kamchatskiy
Sakhalin
Sea of Okhotsk
Khabarovsk
Kodiak
Bethel
Anchorage
Valdez
Providenlya
Anadyr'
Nome
Magadan
Okhotsk
Juneau
Whitehorse
UNITED STATES
Fairbanks
Arctic Circle
Chukchi Sea
Pevek
Cherskiy
Oymyakon
Dawson
Watson Lake
Wrangel Island
Yakutsk
Barrow
Prudhoe Bay
East Siberian Sea
Verkhoyansk
Inuvik
Beaufort Sea
Hay River
Echo Bay
Yellowknife
Tiksi
NEW SIBERIAN ISLANDS
Laptev Sea
Victoria Island
Arctic Ocean
10°C (50°F) isotherm, July
Cambridge Bay
QUEEN ELIZABETH ISLANDS
CANADA
RUSSIA
SEVERNAYA ZEMLYA
North Pole
Kangiqciniq (Rankin Inlet)
Resolute
Repulse Bay
Hudson Bay
Noril'sk
Ellesmere Island
Alert
Dikson
Kara Sea
Qaanaaq (Thule)
FRANZ JOSEF LAND
Baffin Island
Baffin Bay
Nord
Iqaluit (Frobisher Bay)
Longyearbyen
Svalbard (NORWAY)
NOVAYA ZEMLYA
Greenland (DENMARK)
Davis Strait
Barents Sea
Kangerlussuaq (Søndre Strømfjord)
Bjørnøya (NORWAY)
Greenland Sea
Nuuk (Godthåb)
Paamiut (Frederikshåb)
Tasiilaq (Ammassalik)
Narsarsuaq
Ittoqqortoormiit (Scoresbysund)
Jan Mayen (NORWAY)
Murmansk
Arkhangel'sk
Perm'
Labrador Sea
Norwegian Sea
Denmark Strait
Kazan'
Samara
Reykjavík
ICELAND
NORWAY
FINLAND
Nizhniy Novgorod
St. Petersburg
Moscow
Saratov
North Atlantic Ocean
Tórshavn
Faroe Islands (DENMARK)
SWEDEN
Helsinki
Tallinn
Oslo
Stockholm
Riga
LATVIA
Volgograd
Scale 1:39,000,000
Azimuthal Equal-Area Projection
500 Kilometers
500 Miles
SHETLAND ISLANDS
Vilnius
Minsk
BELARUS
Kharkiv
Rostov
Copenhagen
DENMARK
North Sea
Kiev
UKRAINE
The Arctic region is often defined as that area where the average temperature for the warmest month is below 10°C.
Belfast
Warsaw
POLAND
Berlin
GERMANY
Dublin
U.K.
802698AI (R02112) 4-00

CPSIA information can be obtained
at www.ICGtesting.com
Printed in the USA
JSHW022359070623
42845JS00003BA/1

9 781839 989223